BEHIND THE NIMBUS

TRUTH ABOUT ABELISM

WYBENN CLARK SANTOS-CAPIN

Made with ♥ on the Notion Press Platform
www.notionpress.com

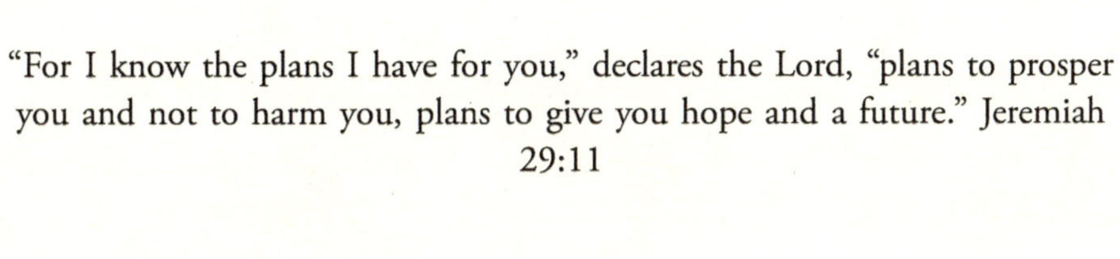

"For I know the plans I have for you," declares the Lord, "plans to prosper you and not to harm you, plans to give you hope and a future." Jeremiah 29:11

Contents

Acknowledgements

I would like to express my deepest appreciation to everyone who played a role in the creation of my book, from writing to publishing.

I am immensely grateful to my dedicated admin assistants: **Maria Isabel Briones** for your invaluable help in writing the first and second chapters., and **Joanne Kris L. Jumawan**, for assisting me to write with chapters three, four, five, six, seven, and eight, and for helping me proofread to publish this book.

I would also like to express my sincere gratitude to **Carl** and **Roxanne** for guiding me back to the Christian community. A special thank you to my discipleship group, **"Fruit Bearers,"** led by our dedicated leader, **JC Montforte**, and to my Christian community in CCF Dubai for your unwavering prayers and support.

I would also like to extend my heartfelt gratitude to my bestfriend, **Dennis Lacson Ledesma**, for financing this book. Without your support, this would not have been possible.

I would also like to express my heartfelt thanks to my brother **Daniel**, to my sister **Caryl,** her husband **Jeff,** and their loving children **CJ, Jhaira,** and **Chloe**, for being a constant source of inspiration in my life.

To my loving parents, **Flordeliza and Virgilio Capin**, thank you for always being there to support me. I love you both very much.

Above all, I give my utmost thanks to **God Almighty** and His Son, **Jesus Christ**, for guiding me and providing me with wisdom throughout this journey.

CHAPTER 1

DARK VALLEY

It's mid-October 2021, and the world is gripped by the fear and uncertainty brought on by the COVID-19 pandemic. The atmosphere is heavy with anxiety as people navigate daily life under the shadow of this invisible threat. I hear echoes of anguish—people screaming and crying in despair as they grapple with the loss of their loved ones. The pain of separation and grief permeates the air, creating an overwhelming sense of sorrow that seems to blanket everything. Everywhere I turn, news reports highlight tragic stories of families torn apart, friends left mourning, and communities struggling to cope. Hospitals are filled to capacity, and the images on our screens are stark reminders of the reality many are facing. It feels as though a collective mourning is unfolding, where each loss is not just a statistic but a deeply personal tragedy.

However, the pain and anxiety brought on by this crisis pale in comparison to my deepest anguish and desperation as I grapple with the total loss of my vision. In those moments, I felt incredibly naive, consumed by thoughts of my situation and the uncertainty of my future. Questions flooded my mind: Who would take care of me if my parents were no longer around? Who would love me and provide the support I so desperately needed? The weight of loneliness pressed heavily on my heart. It seemed that everyone else was preoccupied with their own struggles, caught up in their busy lives, while I felt invisible and isolated. In a world already overwhelmed by fear and loss, my own challenges felt magnified. The isolation deepened my sense of despair, leaving me to wonder if anyone would notice my pain or offer a hand to help me navigate this difficult journey. The fear of being alone in the face of such uncertainty was almost as daunting as the loss itself.I am afraid of what would be my future.

It was precisely midnight, and a thick blanket of darkness enveloped my surroundings, creating an almost suffocating atmosphere. The only sounds breaking the silence were the low growl of thunder and the heavy rain that pounded relentlessly against my window. Each drop echoed like a drumbeat, amplifying the isolation I felt as I lay in my room, wide awake, caught in the throes of my thoughts. The storm outside seemed to resonate with the chaos swirling within me, mirroring my inner turmoil with each rumble of thunder.

My headache fiercely, a persistent throb that refused to subside, intensifying with every flash of lightning that illuminated the night. The flickering light revealed fleeting shadows in my room, casting an eerie glow that heightened my sense of loneliness. It was as if the darkness itself was alive, wrapping around me like a shroud, amplifying my feelings of despair and isolation. I felt like a ghost trapped in my own life, invisible to the world outside.

As I lay there, I couldn't help but feel a deep sadness settle in my heart. It ached, not just from the physical pain, but from a profound sense of loss—loss of peace, joy, and connection. My heart cried out for comfort, for understanding, but all I found was the oppressive weight of solitude. I was utterly alone in this darkened room, and the heavy silence pressed down on me like a thick fog, making it hard to breathe.

With every rumble of thunder, memories flooded my mind—moments of laughter, love, and warmth that felt like distant dreams now. The rain outside seemed to echo my emotions, each drop a tear falling from my weary soul. I longed for a way out, for a glimmer of hope to pierce through the gloom that surrounded me. But instead, I felt trapped in this cycle of darkness, unable to escape the shadows that loomed large in my mind.

I tried to focus on anything else, to ground myself in the present moment. I counted the seconds between the flashes of lightning and the cracks of thunder, hoping to distract myself from the ache within. I listened intently to the rhythm of the rain, attempting to find solace in its familiar sound, but it only served to heighten my sense of despair. The storm outside felt like a mirror reflecting my internal struggles, the chaos outside mirroring the tempest brewing in my heart.

At that stillness, I yearned for connection, for someone to reach out and pull me from this abyss of solitude. I wished for the dawn, a time when the light would break through the darkness and bring clarity, a time when I could emerge from the shadows that felt so consuming. But as the minutes ticked by, the night stretched on, each moment feeling like an eternity.

I closed my eyes, allowing the sounds of the storm to wash over me. I hoped for peace, for an end to the turmoil that had taken root within me.Two hours later, the rain finally ceased, leaving behind an unsettling silence that felt heavy in the stillness. The storm had faded, but in its wake, my surroundings felt eerily quiet, amplifying the sound of my own heart, which pumped rapidly in my chest. Each beat echoed in my ears, a constant reminder of my anxiety and turmoil.

In this silence, unwelcome voices began to emerge from the shadows of my mind, whispering cruelly that I was worthless. They twisted around me like vines, suffocating any flicker of hope that had dared to linger. I fought against these thoughts, desperate to drown them out, yet they persisted, wearing down at my self-worth and fueling my sense of isolation.

As the weight of the silence pressed down on me, I realized that this internal battle was just as fierce as the storm that had raged outside. I felt trapped in a cycle of despair, where the absence of noise only heightened my insecurities. The quiet, once a welcome reprieve, now felt like an echo chamber for my darkest fears. All I could do was breathe and hope that somehow, I would find the strength to silence those voices, to reclaim my sense of self amidst the chaos within.

. I am Wybenn Clark, a name that once resonated with strength and confidence, reflecting my belief in my own capabilities. I've always prided myself on being resilient, on facing challenges head-on with determination and a sense of purpose. But now, it feels as though everything I built is disintegrating before my eyes. I lost my job in Dubai, a place where I had envisioned not just a career but a future filled with promise and growth. That job was more than just a paycheck; it represented my hard work, my ambitions, and the plans I had meticulously crafted for myself.

With the loss of my job came the collapse of my career aspirations and long-term dreams of relocating to Canada. I had envisioned a new life there—one where I could thrive and create a stable, fulfilling future. Now, those dreams feel distant and unattainable, like mirages fading in the desert heat. Financially, I find myself in a precarious position, struggling to make ends meet, and the weight of that burden adds to my sense of hopelessness.

It's a hard pill to swallow, knowing that I once had everything in place and now feel utterly unmoored.

Moreover, I face this difficult chapter in my life without the support of friends or family. I don't have siblings to confide in or friends who can provide a listening ear or a shoulder to lean on. This isolation amplifies my feelings of despair, making it all the more challenging to navigate this storm. In moments of vulnerability, I question my worth and purpose. Who am I without my job, my plans, and the relationships I once took for granted?

The small voices in my mind gradually intensified, morphing into a cacophony of harsh accusations. "You're useless, Wybenn Clark! You're such a burden to your parents! Your life is worthless!" The words reverberated through my thoughts, drowning out any remnants of hope. They echoed relentlessly, a cruel mantra that played on repeat, amplifying my insecurities and fears.

I tossed and turned, desperately seeking respite, but the weight of those voices was suffocating. Sleep eluded me, slipping further away with every harsh syllable that rang in my ears. I felt trapped in a relentless cycle of self-doubt, unable to find even a moment of peace. The darkness of the room mirrored the darkness in my mind, and I could feel the oppressive atmosphere closing in around me.

Each time I tried to quiet the storm within, the voices grew louder, piercing through any attempt at reassurance. It was as if they were feeding off my vulnerability, growing stronger with each passing minute. I lay there, wide awake and restless, consumed by a sense of hopelessness, wondering how to escape this torment that felt like it was slowly unraveling my very sense of self.

I stood up from my bed, a suffocating weight of despair pressing down on me. In that moment, it felt as if my 36 years of existence were utterly devoid of value. I contemplated ending it all, thinking about drinking insecticides or any poisonous liquid that could swiftly erase my pain. The idea wrapped around me like a dark shroud, promising an escape from the relentless suffering that had become my daily reality.

The voices in my mind grew louder, each one more damning than the last: “You’re useless! You’re a burden to your parents! Your life is worthless!” They echoed mercilessly, amplifying my feelings of isolation and hopelessness. Memories of dreams deferred and opportunities lost surged forward, reminding me of the weight of my failures. “I don’t wanna leave, I wanna die”

My room was on the second floor, a space that once felt safe but now felt like a prison. As I opened the door, an overwhelming wave of emotion surged through me, and tears began to spill down my cheeks. My deepest sadness, anxiety, and depression crashed over me like a relentless tide, pushing me toward the thought of ending my life.

Each step down the staircase was heavy, weighted with the cruel reminders of my worthlessness. “You’re a burden to everyone around you,” the voices in my head echoed, each word reverberating in the hollow silence. The stairs felt like an obstacle course of despair, each step a painful reminder of my isolation and the chasm that seemed to widen between me and the world outside.

I gripped the banister, knuckles turning white, fighting against the urge to let go. My heart raced as I descended, torn between the suffocating pull of hopelessness and the faint glimmer of hope that flickered within me. Could I find a way back? The tears that fell were not just an expression of sorrow; they were a plea, a silent cry for understanding in a world that felt so unforgiving.

As I reached the bottom of the stairs, I paused, caught in a moment of reflection. This descent was not just about moving downward physically; it represented a pivotal moment in my life. Would I let the darkness swallow me whole, or could I muster the courage to seek the light, to fight for my life even when every fiber of my being felt like giving in?

I felt an intense anger bubbling inside me—anger toward myself and toward the God who created me. "Why me?" I thought, grappling with the sheer unfairness of my situation. In the depths of my heart, I knew I had always prided myself on being a good person, a devoted servant, and a loving child. I wasn’t a drug addict, a gambler, or a murderer. I followed the rules and respected the law, striving to live my life with integrity and purpose.

Yet, despite my efforts to do right, life had thrown me into a pit of despair that felt utterly undeserved. I watched as others who seemed to embrace chaos and disregard the rules led seemingly happy lives, while I struggled under the weight of my own sorrow. The stark contrast made my anger flare even more intensely. Why was I the one left to suffer? How could a higher power allow someone like me—someone who tried so hard to do everything right—to endure such relentless pain and turmoil?

As those questions churned in my mind, I felt a tempest of confusion and resentment brewing within me. The frustration gnawed at my insides, leading me to question everything: my faith, my choices, and the very fabric of my existence. I wanted answers—clarity and a reason for the suffering that seemed so unjust. It was as if my life had become a cruel joke, a series of unfortunate events that mocked my efforts to be virtuous.

The anger morphed into a heavy weight on my chest, pressing down on me with every breath. I longed for someone to hear my silent screams, to acknowledge the turmoil that raged within. "I've done everything right!" I wanted to shout to the universe. "Why does it feel like I'm being punished?" Each day felt like a battle against the darkness, and I found myself spiraling deeper into despair.

CHAPTER 2

CONTEMPLATING MY SHADOWS

I am Wybenn Clark, and on March 12, 2018, I was celebrating my 34th birthday in Dubai, surrounded by friends and colleagues. The atmosphere was vibrant, filled with joy and laughter as we busily prepared food in the kitchen for my special occasion. The scents of various dishes mingled together, creating a comforting backdrop to the excitement in the air.

Everyone chipped in, chopping vegetables, setting the table, and sharing stories that made us all laugh. It felt like a celebration of not just another year of life but of the bonds we had formed in this bustling city far from home. I was filled with gratitude for the people around me, who turned an ordinary day into something extraordinary. As the preparations unfolded, I couldn't help but reflect on the journey that had brought me here, feeling hopeful and content in that moment of togetherness. I arrived in Dubai in 2015, having left Manila behind in pursuit of a better future. The decision weighed heavily on me, especially as my mother was ill, having been diagnosed with thyroid cancer. My arrival coincided with the midst of Ramadan, a time when many businesses operated on limited hours, often managed remotely by distant bosses. Compounding these challenges was the relentless heat and humidity of Dubai, which made the transition even more daunting.

I was living in flat 109 in Mankhool, Bur Dubai, surrounded by close friends who felt more like family. Among them was Aline, a 39-year-old marketing analyst working in one of the companies in Dubai Healthcare City. Her warmth and laughter always brightened our home. Glenn, 34, had recently celebrated his birthday in February. He worked as a communications engineer in Internet City. His fiancée, Bella, a dedicated nurse at a specialty clinic in Jumeirah Lakes Towers, brought a nurturing presence to our group. Ed, the head of our team and a long-time friend of Aline since their college days, was an inspiring leader with a talent for organizing our gatherings. Finally, there was Dennis, my best friend, 33, an accountant at an oil and gas company in the UAE. We had been together for four years, sharing countless adventures, ambitions, and moments filled with joy. Our flat was a hub of laughter, dreams, and camaraderie, making every day in Dubai feel like a celebration of friendship and life.

That night, I invited a wonderful mix of friends to celebrate my birthday. Marshie, our Christian Life group leader and a dedicated athlete, brought his infectious energy, while his friends Cristy and Yas, both athletes, added to the excitement. Seraphina and her sister Vera, long-time friends of Aline from her previous company in Dubai Internet City, were also there, bringing their charm to the celebration. Lastly, Sally, Aline's best friend who worked as a tutor in Abu Dhabi, completed the group, adding her own warmth and laughter to the gathering.

I also welcomed my close colleagues from the office: John, along with Cyril and her husband JC, and Carmela. Our flat was transformed into a vibrant hub of joy, filled with delicious food, lively music, and the sound of laughter echoing off the walls.

The atmosphere was electric, with conversations flowing freely as everyone mingled, sharing stories and celebrating not just my birthday but the beautiful connections we had built together. It was a night to remember, a perfect blend of friendship, fun, and the spirit of togetherness that made Dubai feel like home.

As I leaned over my birthday cake, ready to blow out the candles, the room filled with the cheerful sounds of “Happy Birthday” from my friends. Just as I took a deep breath, preparing to make my wish, a sudden knock at the door interrupted the moment. Curiosity sparked in the air, and everyone turned to see who it could be.

To my delight, the door swung open to reveal Gina, one of my closest friends and someone who felt like an older sister to me. She stood there with a beaming smile, holding a beautiful cake adorned with candles, her voice joining in with our chorus of “Happy Birthday.” The surprise brought an immediate rush of joy, and the room erupted into cheers.

Gina’s infectious energy filled the space, and as she walked in, her presence made the celebration feel even more special. We embraced, laughter and happiness intertwining as I thanked her for her thoughtful surprise. It was a moment that perfectly captured the essence of friendship, reminding me how fortunate I was to have such wonderful people in my life. The night continued with even more laughter, love, and of course, cake, making it a birthday to remember.

As the evening progressed, we poured drinks and settled into conversations about our future plans. The lively atmosphere buzzed with excitement and a hint of nostalgia. We knew that Dubai, with all its vibrancy, was not a permanent home for any of us—there was no path to residency or citizenship. This reality weighed on our minds as we discussed our dreams and aspirations.

Our talk shifted to the idea of building a foundation for our futures. We spoke about the need to create a stable roof over our heads, to establish ourselves in a place where we could truly belong. Each of us shared our hopes, whether it was starting a business, furthering our careers, or finding new opportunities. The conversation flowed, fueled by laughter and the warmth of our friendship, but there was also a sense of urgency beneath it all.

We envisioned what life could look like beyond Dubai, contemplating the possibility of new cities, new jobs, and even new adventures. The uncertainty of the future felt daunting, but as we raised our glasses to toast to our ambitions, we found comfort in the bonds we had forged. Together, we knew we could navigate whatever came next, making plans while cherishing the moments we had in this beautiful city.

As we sipped our drinks and shared our dreams, the conversation naturally turned to the future. Six years from now, I realized, I would be in my middle years, a pivotal time when I needed to seriously consider my path. Canada emerged as a central topic, a beautiful country brimming with nature and abundant opportunities.

We spoke of its stunning landscapes, from towering mountains to serene lakes, and the promise of a life enriched by outdoor adventures. Canada was not just a destination; it represented hope and possibility—a place where we could build a stable future and truly thrive. The idea of pursuing careers in a country known for its inclusivity and quality of life ignited our imaginations.

With each passing moment, the vision of a new life in Canada felt more tangible. We discussed the potential for personal and professional growth, the chance to settle down in a welcoming community, and the prospect of crafting a life that was not only fulfilling but also sustainable. At moment, amidst laughter and camaraderie, we all agreed: Canada felt like the best choice for our dreams, a beacon guiding us toward a brighter future.

A month after my birthday, fueled by our discussions and dreams of a brighter future, Dennis, Gina, and I made the decision to explore our options for immigrating to Canada. Our excitement was palpable, but so was the nervousness that accompanied such a significant life change. We knew this was a pivotal moment in our journey.

We visited a consultancy agency located on Sheikh Zayed Road, conveniently situated across from the World Trade Center and near the Metro Station. As we walked through the bustling streets, anticipation bubbled within us, mingling with the reality of what we were about to undertake.

Upon entering the office of Strata, one of the leading immigration consultancy services in Dubai, we were greeted by a warm and professional atmosphere. The agency specialized in helping individuals obtain permanent residency not just in Canada, but also in the USA, UK, Australia, and New Zealand.

As we settled into the consultation room, our hearts raced with a mixture of hope and apprehension. We knew that this step could change the course of our lives. The consultant began to explain the various pathways to residency, detailing the requirements and processes involved. Listening intently, we exchanged glances, silently acknowledging the significance of this moment. This was not just an application; it was the first step toward our dream of building a new life in Canada—a life filled with opportunity, adventure, and the promise of belonging.

After our pre-screening consultation, the excitement and anticipation grew stronger. We felt a sense of relief and determination as we made the decision to move forward with our immigration journey. With a mix of nervousness and exhilaration, we completed our first payment, marking an important milestone in our quest for a new life.

As part of the process, we received a packet of documentation and a certificate that officially recognized our intent to pursue permanent residency. Holding those papers in our hands felt monumental; they represented our dreams taking shape and the promise of a future we had long envisioned.

With the initial steps behind us, we knew our next move was crucial: compiling the rest of the necessary documentation. The list was extensive—everything from proof of employment and financial statements to IELTS and character references.

Three months later, my thoughts turned to an important milestone: my mother's 60th birthday, which I would be celebrating back in the Philippines. It felt imperative to be there for her, to honor this special occasion and share my journey with her in person. However, before I could pack my bags, I needed to prepare all my reports and audits as quickly and efficiently as possible.

Working as an external auditor for UK banks, meant that my workload was often heavy, filled with intricate details and tight deadlines. Despite the pressure mounting around me, I remained optimistic. I knew that if I focused and organized my tasks, I could complete everything in time to take a short-term leave from work.

I dedicated myself to crafting concise and thorough reports, pouring my energy into each line item while keeping my goal in mind. The thought of surprising my mother with news of my plans to migrate to Canada kept me motivated. I imagined her reaction—the joy and pride in her eyes as I shared my dreams for a new beginning.

Each completed report brought me one step closer to that moment, fueling my determination to finish strong. As I navigated the busy days ahead, I found comfort in the knowledge that this trip was not just about celebrating her birthday; it was about sharing a pivotal chapter of my life with the woman who had always supported me.

I've always considered myself a workaholic, fiercely dedicated to my career as an auditor. My focus extended beyond just my job; I also felt a deep responsibility toward my family back in the Philippines and my newly founded business, Jetliner Express Travel and Tours. Balancing these aspects of my life was no small feat, but I was determined to make it work.

I took pride in my capabilities, often likening myself to Superman—capable of tackling any challenge that came my way. The name Clark even felt like a badge of honor, reminding me of my strength and resilience. Whether it was meeting tight deadlines at work, supporting my family, or nurturing my travel agency, I thrived on the hustle and bustle.

Each day presented a new opportunity to push my limits, and I relished the idea of achieving my goals. I knew that my hard work and ambition would eventually pay off, leading me toward a future filled with possibilities. Balancing my roles felt like a thrilling adventure, one that I embraced wholeheartedly, proud of the progress I was making in every facet of my life.

On July 4, I submitted my request to my manager for a short vacation to attend my mother's 60th birthday. After much anticipation, she reluctantly agreed, but only allowed me to take three days off. It was frustrating, given the workload piling up at the office, but I didn't have much choice. I was determined to be there for my mother's special day, no matter the constraints.

I quickly booked my flight with Cebu Pacific, choosing July 14 as my departure date. The excitement of the upcoming reunion fueled me as I packed my bags, though I couldn't shake the exhaustion from my busy schedule. After a long journey, I arrived in Manila the following day, greeted by the familiar chaos of the airport.

I had a five-hour layover in Manila before catching my next flight to Cebu. As I navigated the terminal, fatigue threatened to weigh me down, but my heart was brimming with excitement. I could already envision the look on my mother's face when she saw me. The anticipation kept me alert, even as I fought off sleepiness. Each passing hour brought me closer to celebrating not just her milestone birthday, but also sharing my dreams and plans for the future. It felt like a journey not only to mark a special occasion but to reconnect with my roots and the people I loved most.

I finally arrived in Cebu just after midday, my heart racing with anticipation as I took a cab heading to our home in Liloan. The familiar sights of the island brought back memories, but nothing could compare to the moment I stepped through the door. My mother welcomed me with pure joy, her face lighting up with surprise and happiness as she embraced me tightly. Atthat moment, I felt an overwhelming sense of belonging, as if all the distance and effort had been worth it.

We had planned her special day at a nearby mountain resort, just two miles from home, where we would celebrate with distant relatives, family, and friends. The excitement was palpable as we made our way to the venue, the air filled with laughter and chatter. The lush surroundings and breathtaking views set the perfect backdrop for this milestone celebration.

As we arrived, I took a moment to soak it all in—the decorations, the familiar faces, and the warm atmosphere that enveloped us. It was more than just a birthday party; it was a gathering of love and connection, a testament to the bonds that held us together despite the miles apart. I couldn't wait to share my plans for Canada with my mother and to create unforgettable memories on this special day.

Tomorrow, I will be flying back to Dubai, marking the end of this heartwarming visit. As I prepared for the long journey ahead, I knew I had to share my good news with my mother—it was my birthday gift to her. I could hardly contain my excitement as I revealed my immigration plans to Canada.

Her reaction was everything I had hoped for; she was overjoyed, her eyes sparkling with pride. I remembered her words clearly: "Wherever you go, that's also my achievement." It filled me with warmth to know that my dreams were intertwined with hers, and her unwavering support meant the world to me.

I took a moment to express my gratitude, thanking her for always providing me with assurance and approval in all my life's plans. Her belief in me had been a guiding light through every challenge I faced. As we embraced, I felt a deep connection, knowing that no matter where I went, I carried her love and encouragement with me. It was a bittersweet moment, but I left feeling stronger, ready to tackle whatever lay ahead.

After my short visit to the Philippines, I returned to work, diving headfirst into my backlog of tasks. Juggling my responsibilities as an external auditor and my travel agency, Jetliner Express Travel and Tours, kept me busy. I found myself working late into the night, often sleeping only about three hours, which I somehow managed to function on. However, there was one thing I noticed about my body. I began feeling a heaviness in my chest, which I initially thought was just a simple muscle pain. I ignored it for a few weeks, but the discomfort soon worsened. What started as mild chest pain turned into a heavy sensation, like two concrete blocks pressing down on my chest. At times, it became difficult to breathe, yet I continued to work, pushing aside the signals my body was trying to send me.

While crafting quotations for customers, I also dedicated time to developing internal procedures for Jetliner Express. I knew that establishing solid foundations was crucial for the agency's success. Additionally, I was in the process of building a website to showcase our offerings to potential clients, wanting to create an inviting platform that would attract and engage them.

Despite the exhaustion, I felt a surge of motivation with each completed task. The thrill of entrepreneurship, coupled with my commitment to my career, fueled my determination. I envisioned the growth of my travel agency and the opportunities it would bring, and that vision kept me pushing through the late nights. Balancing everything was challenging, but I was driven by the desire to turn my dreams into reality.

On October 28 of that same year, around eight o'clock in the morning, I was supposed to wake up and prepare for work. But something terrifying happened. I thought it was still evening when I opened my eyes to total darkness. I couldn't see a single light, and my heart began to race. Fear gripped me, leaving me unsure of what to do. I closed my eyes, hoping it was all just a dream.

I opened my eyes slowly, but everything remained shrouded in darkness. I waited for about five minutes, and gradually, a faint light began to emerge, though it wasn't the same as before. I could see dark spots and flashes, and an unsettling realization dawned on me: something was wrong. Fear gripped me at the thought of losing my eyesight; my vision was fading to gray, and I struggled to make out the letters on my reports. "Lord, what is happening to me?" I whispered, panic rising within me. Panic set in, my hands and body trembling uncontrollably. I shouted for help, and thank God, Gina and Dennis were there. Dennis wanted to assist me, but he was on the verge of leaving for work and had a business meeting to attend. Fortunately, Gina was available; she wasn't working at the moment and was still hunting for a new job. Gina was in the kitchen preparing breakfast when I shouted for help. She immediately rushed over, her own panic evident. Turning to Dennis, she asked what we should do. He suggested we call the nearest hospital. We quickly searched online, and fortunately, Gina found a number to call. She reached out to Moorfields Hospital in Dubai Healthcare City, which specializes in eyecare.

We stepped out of our building, the chilly air hitting me like a splash of cold water. Gina, her face pale and strained, quickly called a taxi. As we waited, I could feel the tension building between us. A few minutes later, a taxi pulled up, and Gina hurried to help me inside, holding her left arm for support.

As we drove through the Dubai Healthcare City, my gaze flickered from the passing scenery to Gina's worried expression. I couldn't help but feel a knot of anxiety tighten in my stomach. The streets blurred past, and I struggled to keep my thoughts organized.

I was overwhelmed by the weight of uncertainty. Should I be at work right now, checking in with my manager about my absence? Or was it more important to focus on my and find out what was happening with me? The thought of having to explain everything to my boss felt daunting, especially when my mind was racing with worry.

Every jolt of the taxi sent shockwaves through me, and I clenched my jaw, trying to maintain my composure. "What if this is serious?" I thought. "Just hold on, okay?" I said, attempting to offer some reassurance for myself, though I wasn't sure if I believed it myself. The anxiety kept spiraling, and I realized I wasn't thinking clearly. My heart raced, and my palms grew clammy.

At that moment, all I could do was focus on the fact that we were on our way to the hospital. I took a deep breath, reminding myself that we would face whatever was ahead together.

As I stepped into the lobby of the eye specialty clinic at Moorfields Hospital, a wave of relief washed over me. The bright lights and bustling atmosphere felt both foreign and familiar, grounding me in the reality of the situation. It was then that my mind finally made a decision—I needed to call my manager and request sick leave.

With Gina by my side, I took a deep breath and pulled out my phone. "Can you help me with this?" I asked, my voice barely above a whisper. She nodded, her own worry momentarily set aside as she focused on supporting me. Together, we crafted a message through WhatsApp, her calm demeanor guiding me through the words I struggled to find.

Gina suggested I explain my situation clearly but briefly. "I'm feeling unwell and need to visit the hospital for an urgent check-up. I'll keep you updated on my condition."

Gina glanced at me, reassuringly nodding as she hit send. The message disappeared into the digital ether, leaving me with a sense of uncertainty. What would my manager say? Would he understand? I felt vulnerable, but I knew I had to prioritize my health.

As we waited for a response, I glanced around the lobby. The atmosphere was a mix of anxious faces and busy staff, all navigating their own challenges. At that moment, I realized I wasn't alone in this; everyone around me was fighting their own battles.

A few minutes later, a member of the clinic staff approached us, clipboard in hand, ready to gather my personal information. They asked about my medical history and current condition, their tone professional yet compassionate. I answered their questions as best as I could, trying to keep my voice steady despite the whirlwind of anxiety in my chest.

Once they had taken down my details, another nurse came to guide me to the laboratory examination room. As we walked down the corridor, I felt a flicker of hope—perhaps this was just a minor issue, something that could be quickly resolved. Gina walked alongside me, her presence a comforting anchor in the midst of my swirling thoughts.

When we arrived at the examination room, I took a deep breath and stepped inside. The room was bright and sterile, filled with the hum of medical equipment. I was directed to sit down in the patient chair, and as I did, my heart began to race. I could feel it pounding in my chest, each beat a reminder of my worries.

I closed my eyes for a moment, praying silently to God. "Please let this be nothing serious," I whispered in my mind. I longed for reassurance, for the strength to get through whatever lay ahead. The hope that this would all be just a small bump in the road kept me grounded as I prepared for the examination.

Gina sat nearby, her eyes filled with concern but also a quiet determination to be there for me. With her by my side, I felt a little more at ease, ready to face whatever news awaited us.

After a series of examinations, I returned to the waiting lounge, my mind swirling with uncertainty about what would come next. Time seemed to stretch on endlessly; I checked the clock repeatedly, each tick amplifying my anxiety. About an hour and a half later, my name was finally called by a member of the clinic staff. Her name tag read "Vien," and she greeted me with a warm smile that offered a small comfort in the tense atmosphere.

"Follow me, please," she said, guiding me to room 204. As I entered, I was met by Dr. Muhammad, a VR retina surgeon with a calm demeanor that immediately put me at ease. He introduced himself and began to examine my eyes, asking questions about my vision and the issues I had been experiencing. I explained how my eyesight had become increasingly blurry, and the worry that had been gnawing at me for days.

Dr. Muhammad listened intently, then made a call to another doctor, requesting her presence in the room. My heart raced as I waited, unsure of what was happening. Moments later, Dr. Amanda entered, holding the laboratory test results in her hands. She looked serious yet compassionate as she prepared to explain my condition.

"Based on the results," she began, "you have been diagnosed with diabetic retinopathy. Your retina is starting to bleed and detach from its original position, which is causing the blurry vision."

Her words felt like a heavy weight dropping into my stomach. I glanced at Gina, who looked equally concerned, her grip on my hand tightening. Dr. Amanda continued, her tone steady. "Additionally, your blood pressure has risen to 195 over 142, and your blood sugar level is alarmingly high at 400 mg/dL. This combination is critical and requires immediate attention."

A wave of fear washed over me. The implications of her words began to sink in, and I realized that this was more serious than I had hoped. I felt overwhelmed by the reality of my situation, but I also knew I needed to focus. With Gina by my side, I took a deep breath, steeling myself for the next steps in this unexpected journey.

I felt a wave of emotion crash over me, and tears began to flow. The diagnosis felt like a heavy burden, leaving me feeling hopeless and overwhelmed. So many questions flooded my mind, each one more pressing than the last. Should I stay here in Dubai and go through with the eye operation, or should I return to my home country to have the procedure done there?

The thought of leaving the familiar surroundings of this clinic felt daunting. I had grown accustomed to the bustling city and the support of friends like Gina, who stood by me through this crisis. Yet, the idea of returning home brought its own sense of comfort—family, familiarity, and perhaps a sense of security that felt lost in the uncertainty of my situation.

"Gina," I choked out between sobs, "what do you think I should do?" My voice trembled, revealing just how fragile I felt in that moment. I needed guidance, someone to help me navigate this maze of decisions.

She leaned closer, her eyes filled with empathy. "We'll figure it out together," she assured me. "You don't have to make this choice alone." Her words were a lifeline, grounding me when I felt like I was drifting away.

As I wiped my tears, I began to consider my options more clearly. The urgency of my condition was undeniable, and I needed to act quickly. But the fear of undergoing such a significant operation in an unfamiliar place loomed over me, making it hard to think straight.

"Maybe we can get a second opinion," I suggested hesitantly, hoping that more information would help ease my anxiety. "I want to be sure about what to do next."

Gina nodded, her determination evident. "That sounds like a good plan. Let's gather all the information we can before making a decision."

With that, I felt a flicker of hope amidst the uncertainty. I knew I wasn't alone in this fight, and together, we would face whatever came next.

Dr. Muhammad approached me with a sense of urgency that was hard to ignore. "We need to discuss your options," he said, his expression serious. "Given your diagnosis, you need to undergo eye surgery immediately. It's crucial that we act quickly."

My heart sank as I processed his words. "How soon?" I asked, my voice barely above a whisper.

"You have fourteen days to make a decision," he replied, his tone firm yet compassionate. "If we don't proceed with the operation at that timeframe, the tissues in your eye could deteriorate further, potentially leading to irreversible damage."

A chill ran down my spine. Fourteen days didn't feel like nearly enough time to weigh my options, especially given the gravity of the situation. The thought of losing my vision was terrifying, but the idea of rushing into a decision without fully understanding the consequences made me feel even more lost.

"Dr. Muhammad," I said, my voice trembling, "can you explain what the surgery will involve? I need to know what I'm facing."

He nodded, taking a moment to gather his thoughts. "The surgery will aim to repair the damage to your retina and stop the bleeding. It's a delicate procedure, but we've had success with patients in similar situations. However, the longer we wait, the more risk there is to your vision."

As he spoke, my mind raced with fears and possibilities. I glanced at Gina, who was listening intently, her expression a mix of concern and support. I could feel the weight of the decision pressing down on me, and I realized how critical it was to gather as much information as possible in the days ahead.

"Thank you, Dr. Muhammad," I said, trying to steady my voice. "I appreciate your help. I'll need some time to think about this and discuss it further."

"Of course," he replied. "Take the time you need, but remember, time is of the essence."

As he left the room, I felt a mixture of fear and determination. I had a lot to consider in the next two weeks, but I was determined to make the best decision for my health and my future.

Dr. Amanda continued, her voice calm but firm. "Before we proceed with the surgery, it's crucial that we get your blood pressure and blood sugar levels under control. Both need to be within a normal range to minimize any risks during the operation."

She handed me a printed program outlining a one- to two-week plan, designed to help me achieve those goals. "This should give you enough time to make the necessary adjustments," she explained, pointing to dietary recommendations, exercise routines, and regular monitoring tips.

As I glanced at the program, a mixture of relief and apprehension washed over me. I knew that taking these steps was vital, but the thought of making such significant lifestyle changes in a short time felt daunting.

"Where should I go for support?" I asked, eager to start this process.

Dr. Amanda smiled and replied, "I'm referring you to Jupiter Specialty Clinic, which is conveniently located just six hundred meters from your building. It's very accessible, and you should be able to visit regularly for follow-ups and guidance."

The news brought a small sense of comfort. Knowing that I had a nearby clinic made the task ahead seem less overwhelming. "Thank you," I said, feeling a flicker of hope. "I'll make sure to stick to the program."

As I left the room, my mind was a whirlwind of confusion and fear. I felt overwhelmed by the flood of information from my doctors, struggling to process everything they had just shared. "I can't believe this is happening to me," I thought, each step feeling heavier than the last.

Gina, sensing my turmoil, suggested, "Maybe you should call your family in the Philippines and share what's going on. They might want to know."

I hesitated, knowing how difficult it would be for my mother to hear this news. Just last July, she had turned sixty, and even though her doctors had declared her cancer-free from thyroid cancer, I was acutely aware of how vulnerable her health was. The thought of adding more worry to her life felt unbearable.

Instead, I decided to call my older sister, Caryl. I needed someone to lean on, someone who could understand. As the phone rang, I felt a mix of hope and apprehension. When she finally answered, I quickly explained my current condition, detailing the diagnosis and the urgency of my situation.

But to my dismay, Caryl's response was anything but empathetic. "What? I can't help you. You know I don't have a job," she said, her tone sharp and dismissive. "Okay, I'll talk to Mama."

My heart sank. I had hoped for support, for some sign that I wasn't alone in this battle. Instead, I felt a wave of desperation wash over me. I was losing faith and hope, feeling as if the very people I needed most were unable to offer the comfort I craved.

CHAPTER 3

CATALYST OF DESPAIR

It was the afternoon of November 8, and as I stood in my room, surrounded by my packed bags, I felt an overwhelming sense of unease. Today was the day of my flight back to the Philippines for good. I had submitted my immediate resignation and received my work visa cancellation in just two days, thanks to Irene Santerin—a good friend and a long-time friend of Aline. She had helped me navigate the complexities at DMCC with such kindness, but now, as I prepared to leave, I felt anything but ready, but not emotionally.

While I clung to a thread of hope that I would be back to work after six months of treatment, doubt gnawed at me. "What if the surgery doesn't go as planned?" The thought sent chills down my spine. What would happen if the procedure turned unsuccessful? The unknown loomed large, casting a shadow over my future.

My financial situation added to my anxiety. My gratuity and savings were limited, and the weight of those numbers hung heavily in my mind. "What if my funds aren't enough to cover my treatment? How will I sustain myself?" The fear of spiraling into debt or being unable to afford the care I needed felt suffocating.

I was also plagued by deeper questions that seemed to swirl endlessly. "Who will support me through this? What will my future look like if I can't regain my health?" I thought of my aging parents back home, of the responsibilities I felt towards them, and the uncertainty of how I would care for myself as I grew older. "Who will take care of me when I get old?"

With each thought, a wave of despair washed over me, and I could feel the weight of the world pressing down on my shoulders. I took a deep breath, trying to ground myself in the present moment. I had made this choice for my health, for a chance at a better future, but the path ahead felt riddled with obstacles.

The memories of my visit to Moorfields Hospital lingered vividly in my mind, the weight of that day heavy on my heart. After my appointments, Gina and I returned home, but instead of relief, I was consumed by sadness. I cried for most of the day, sitting on the couch, feeling as if the world had closed in around me.

I knew I had to share this news with my friends, my manager, and my housemates. The thought of opening up about my diagnosis was daunting, but I couldn't keep it to myself any longer.

That afternoon, Dennis called, eager to know the results of my check-ups. When I broke the news, his shock was palpable. "We need to have a meeting at home," he said firmly, his voice tinged with concern. I appreciated his support, but the thought of gathering everyone only amplified my anxiety.

After dinner, we all settled down together. Ed, the head of our friendship group—affectionately dubbed Teambless—took the lead. She had a way of commanding attention, and as she looked around the room, I could see the confusion written on everyone's faces. Bella, Glen, Cristy, Aline, and Dennis were there, each wearing expressions that mirrored my own fears.

Gina sat beside me, her presence a comforting reminder that I wasn't alone in this. Ed positioned herself in front of me, her eyes steady and reassuring. "We're all here for you," she said gently, but I could see the concern etched in her features.

As they began to ask questions, I felt a wave of emotions crash over me—fear, vulnerability, but also a sense of solidarity. I knew these friends would support me, yet the uncertainty of what lay ahead still loomed large.

"Let's talk about what this means for you and how we can help," Ed continued, her voice firm yet compassionate. I took a deep breath, ready to share my story, grateful to have such a strong network around me as I faced this daunting chapter of my life.

As I gathered my thoughts, I took a deep breath and began to explain everything that had happened at the hospital. I shared the diagnosis, the urgency of the situation, and the terrifying possibility of losing my vision permanently. My voice trembled as I spoke, and I could see the concern deepening in the faces of my friends.

They listened intently, their expressions filled with compassion and sadness. Each question I answered seemed to weigh heavier on my heart. When it came time to discuss my options—whether to undergo the operation here in Dubai or return to the Philippines for surgery—I could feel the support surrounding me, a cocoon of love and understanding.

Ed, always the pillar of strength, was the first to react. As I finished speaking, she stood up and enveloped me in a tight hug, tears streaming down her face. "We're going to get through this together," she whispered, her voice choked with emotion. At that moment, I felt a profound sense of connection, but it also magnified my sadness. The thought of leaving this family, my Dubai family, weighed heavily on my heart.

I glanced around the room, seeing the tear-streaked faces of Glen, Aline, and Dennis. Each one of them was grappling with the reality of my situation, their love and concern evident in their eyes. The idea of leaving them, of stepping away from this supportive community, felt unbearable.

"I don't want to leave you all," I admitted, my voice breaking. "You've been my strength through everything."

Dennis and Aline squeezed my hand tightly, a silent reminder that I wasn't alone. "You have to do what's best for your health," she said gently, but I could hear the pain in her voice as well.

The room was filled with an atmosphere of shared sorrow and determination. We discussed the options, weighing the pros and cons, but ultimately, the decision felt like it was looming over me, just out of reach. I knew I needed to focus on my health, but the thought of being separated from the people who had become my family in Dubai was almost too much to bear.

At that moment, surrounded by love, I realized that no matter what I chose, I would carry this bond with me. And while the path ahead felt daunting, I was grateful for their unwavering support as I faced the challenges ahead.

That night was incredibly special to me, a bittersweet mix of emotions swirling around as I realized I needed to focus on getting home to the Philippines as quickly as possible to start my treatment. The weight of my situation hung heavy in the air, but there was also a glimmer of hope—I was determined to fight.

As I continued packing my remaining belongings, each item felt like a reminder of my time in Dubai. Memories flooded my mind, and with them came an overwhelming sense of loss. Tears began to fall as I struggled to hold back my emotions. "Lord, give me strength! Lord, give me strength!" I whispered, my voice choked with desperation.

In those moments, I felt vulnerable, grappling with the reality of what lay ahead. I knew I had to summon every ounce of courage within me, but the fear of the unknown loomed large. I closed my eyes, allowing the tears to flow freely, hoping that my prayers would be heard.

The thought of leaving my Dubai family behind made my heart ache. Yet, I reminded myself that this was a necessary step for my health. I had to trust that I was making the right decision, not just for myself but for everyone who cared about me.

As I wiped my tears, I felt a renewed sense of determination. I was not alone in this fight; I had the love and support of my friends, and I would carry that with me as I embarked on this challenging journey.

With each item I packed, I also packed away my fears, telling myself that I would return stronger. I would do everything in my power to overcome this, and I would be back, ready to reunite with the people who had become my second family.

A few hours later, Dennis came into my room with a sense of urgency. "It's time to get ready," he said gently but firmly. "Don't forget your passport and the cancellation papers for immigration." His practical approach grounded me amidst the whirlwind of emotions I was experiencing.

As he called a taxi to take us to the airport, I felt a mixture of gratitude and sadness. My friends—Gina, Ed, Cristy , Aline, Glenn, and Bella—were all there to support me, each one bringing their own light to this heavy moment. Their presence filled the air with positivity, a stark contrast to the anxiety that had been weighing on me.

When we arrived at the Emirates check-in counter, the reality of the situation began to sink in. Ed and Dennis quickly made their way to the special counter for disabled passengers, where they requested a wheelchair and assistance for me. I appreciated their thoughtfulness, knowing that navigating the airport could be challenging.

As I stood in line, I glanced around at my friends gathered together, their faces a mix of encouragement and sadness. Each of them was doing their best to keep the atmosphere light, sharing jokes and memories of our time together. I felt a surge of love and support, and despite the fear gnawing at my heart, I found comfort in knowing I was not alone.

When it was finally my turn at the check-in counter, I took a deep breath, ready to face the next step of my journey. I could hear Ed and Dennis organizing everything behind me, their voices full of determination and care. They had made sure I was equipped for this journey, not just physically but emotionally as well.

As I prepared to board the flight, I held on to the belief that this was just the beginning of my healing journey. With my friends by my side, I felt a little stronger, ready to take on whatever challenges lay ahead.

The Emirates flight from Dubai to Cebu lasted about nine hours, but for me, it felt like an eternity. As the plane soared through the clouds, I leaned my head against the window, gazing out at the endless expanse of sky. At first, I tried to focus on the positive aspects of my journey—my friends' unwavering support and the hope of returning home for treatment. But soon, those thoughts began to fade, giving way to a deep sadness that enveloped me like a heavy fog.

I felt emotionally drained, each wave of turbulence mirroring the turmoil within me. I couldn't think straight; my mind raced with worries and fears. "What if the surgery doesn't go well? What if I can't regain my vision?" Each thought spiraled further into negativity, and I found myself crying quietly, the tears flowing freely as I tried to process everything.It was as if the weight of my situation had finally crashed down on me at that confined space. The hum of the airplane engines faded into the background as I surrendered to my emotions, feeling utterly lost and alone despite being surrounded by fellow passengers.

As the hours stretched on, I realized this was the beginning of a sleepless night. The combination of anxiety and uncertainty gnawed at me, making it hard to find any comfort in my surroundings. I could feel the heaviness in my heart, a constant reminder of the challenges that awaited me upon my arrival.With every tear that fell, I was letting go of the fear and sadness, but it also felt like I was losing a part of myself—the part that had thrived in Dubai, surrounded by friends and laughter. As the flight continued, I hoped that somewhere along the way, I would find the strength to embrace the next chapter of my life.

CHAPTER 4

EXPERIENCING UTTER RUIN

I formally arrived at Mactan Cebu International Airport on November 9 at 4:30 in the afternoon. As I sat in my seat, waiting for the airport staff to guide me through the process, I couldn't shake the feeling of anxiety building within me. Time passed, and soon I realized I was still sitting there while the other passengers had disembarked. It became clear that no one was coming for me; I had been forgotten.

With a mix of determination and frustration, I gathered my things and prepared to leave the plane on my own. This unexpected challenge greeted me as I stepped into my home country for a few months. I could feel the weight of my luggage—both physically and emotionally—pulling me down as I walked carefully towards the immigration counter, my heart racing with each step.

Once I reached the immigration area, I joined the long line of travelers. My hands were full with my bags, and I felt the sweat beginning to form on my brow. As I waited, an immigration officer approached me, handing me an arrival card and gesturing for me to fill it out. But when I looked at the small sheet of paper, the letters seemed to blur together. The stress of the day had taken its toll, and I found myself struggling to focus.

Feeling overwhelmed, I made a split-second decision and hurried towards the men's restroom. I needed a moment to compose myself. As I entered a cubicle, I leaned against the wall, my hands shaking. I closed my eyes and took a deep breath, fighting against the wave of frustration that washed over me. Why was this so difficult? I had imagined a smooth return, filled with warm embraces and familiar sights, but instead, I was standing alone, lost in my own thoughts.

Inside that restroom, I allowed myself to vent silently. I thought of the family and friends I was eager to see, the memories I hoped to create, and the adventures that awaited me. I reminded myself that this moment was just a small bump in my journey. I could handle it. After a few moments of contemplation, I emerged from the restroom, feeling slightly more grounded. I took another deep breath, squared my shoulders, and rejoined the line at immigration.

As I was finally navigating through the immigration process, another personnel approached me with a warm smile. "Are you okay?" she asked, her voice filled with genuine concern. I sighed with relief at her kindness. "I was waiting for an airport staff to assist me, but nobody came," I explained. "So I decided to walk on my own."

Her expression shifted to one of empathy. "I'm so sorry for that! Let me help you," she said, and from that moment on, she guided me through the remaining steps with efficiency and care. I felt a wave of gratitude wash over me as she walked alongside me, ensuring that I had everything I needed to get through customs and immigration smoothly. After what felt like an eternity, we finally reached the arrival hall of Terminal Two. As I stood there, taking a moment to catch my breath and absorb the surroundings, my heart raced with anticipation. Then, in the distance, I spotted my mother. She was making her way towards me, her face lighting up with joy.

As soon as we were close enough, she wrapped her arms around me, enveloping me in a warm hug that made all the challenges of the day fade away. "Welcome home!" she exclaimed, her voice filled with emotion. I could feel the love radiating from her, and it brought a smile to my face despite everything.

Behind her, I noticed my father waiting in our brand new red sedan, parked just outside. He was chatting with my Aunt Liza, who waved enthusiastically. My younger brother Daniel stood next to them, bouncing on his toes with excitement, his grin wide and infectious.

The sight of my family filled me with warmth and happiness. Despite the rough start to my journey, I was finally home. As I stepped out of the terminal, my mother took my hand, and together we walked toward the car, ready to embrace all the moments we would share together.

It was around six-thirty in the evening when we finally arrived in Liloan, a charming town near the city center and my mother's hometown. The familiar sights and sounds enveloped me as we drove through the streets, stirring up fond memories of my childhood. As we pulled into our driveway, I could hardly contain my excitement.

Stepping out of the car, I was greeted by the cheerful faces of my older sister Caryl and my brother-in-law. They stood at the front door, flanked by my adorable nephews, Chloe and CJ, and my only niece, Jairah. The moment I approached, they rushed forward, wrapping me in a warm welcome that instantly made me feel at home. Caryl pulled me into a tight hug, her voice filled with warmth as she said, " I'll always be here to guide you." Her reassurance was comforting, especially after the chaos of my journey.

Once the hugs settled down, she looked at me with genuine curiosity, her eyes sparkling. "But first, I want to hear everything about your time in Dubai!"

As we walked toward the house, I began to share my situation that time when I was rushed to the hospital, the challenges I faced, and unexpected moments. My family listened intently, their faces reflecting a mix of concern and support. I felt a sense of relief in being able to share my story with them, knowing they were eager to understand what I had been through. I was finally home, surrounded by the people I loved most, ready to embark on this new chapter together.

A few hours after dinner, I walked toward my room, a sense of mixed emotions swirling within me. The familiar scent of home wrapped around me like a warm blanket, yet there was an undeniable tug in my heart. I felt a rush of memories from Dubai coursing through my veins—laughter with friends, the vibrant streets, and the beautiful skyline that seemed to touch the stars.

As I began unpacking my things, each item held a memory: the colorful souvenirs from the markets, the little trinkets that echoed the moments we shared. I arranged my belongings in the cabinet, each piece finding its place like fragments of my life. Still, my soul felt tethered to Dubai, lingering in the warmth of friendships that felt distant now.

Lying on my bed, exhaustion settled over me, but sleep evaded me. The memories played like a slideshow in my mind—the nights spent under the stars, conversations that stretched until dawn, and the bittersweet farewells that lingered long after I boarded the plane. I closed my eyes, wishing my friends were just a few steps away, ready to reminisce and share laughter again.

Just as I began to drift off, a strong wind howled outside, rattling the windows. I jolted awake, heart racing, not merely from the thunderstorm but from a deeper anxiety about what the future held. I reached for my phone, the glow illuminating my worried face as I checked my bank account. The numbers were stark, a reminder of the limited funds I had, and the weight of upcoming operations and medications loomed heavily in my mind.

At that moment, I felt the weight of uncertainty pressing down on me. I thought about the choices I had to make, the path I had to forget, and the challenges I had yet to face. But amidst the fear, a flicker of determination ignited within me. I remembered the resilience I had found in Dubai, how my friends had encouraged me to push through difficulties. I could do this.

As the rain pattered against the window, I took a deep breath, letting the sound soothe my anxious thoughts. I would allow myself to feel the uncertainty, but I wouldn't let it define me. I would embrace the journey ahead, knowing that while the path might be winding and unpredictable, I wasn't walking it alone. With that resolve, I finally drifted into a restless sleep, dreaming of the vibrant streets of Dubai, but also of the promise of new beginnings waiting for me at home.

A few weeks passed since my return home, and the uncertainty about my health began to weigh heavily on my mind. I made my way to Cebu Doctors Hospital in Cebu City, clutching the hope that maybe, just maybe, I could find answers about the state of my eyes—specifically, the damage to my retina that had been a source of anxiety for far too long.

The early morning sun had barely risen when I arrived, its rays casting a warm glow over the bustling city. I navigated through the hospital corridors, the sterile smell of antiseptics mingling with the faint sounds of medical equipment. After what felt like an eternity, I finally spoke with a medical practitioners associated with Dr. Larrazabal. He reviewed my case and, with a sympathetic look, directed me to Chong Hua Hospital, where specialists could provide more focused care.

Frustration bubbled within me. I had woken up early, navigated the chaos of the city, and endured a series of tests—all for what felt like a dead end. I tried to calm myself as I thought about the cost. The laboratory tests at Cebu Doctors Hospital had set me back around 15,000 pesos. I felt the weight of that expense heavy on my shoulders, especially when the results yielded no clear answers.

Days passed, and the anxiety gnawed at me. I finally made my way to Chong Hua Hospital's Eye Institute, where I hoped that this time would be different. The familiar routine unfolded—waiting in line, filling out forms, and enduring another series of tests. This time, the bills piled up even higher, totaling around 20,000 pesos. I tried to reassure myself that this investment might finally lead to clarity and, ultimately, help.

After what felt like hours, I was called in for my consultation. The specialist was thorough, his eyes focused and determined. As Dr. Lim examined my eyes, I held my breath, silently praying for good news. He explained the intricacies of my condition, his voice steady and reassuring. For the first time in weeks, I felt a glimmer of hope. He outlined a potential treatment plan, discussing options that had previously seemed out of reach.

However, as I sat in the office with Dr. Lim, the reality of my situation hit me like a tidal wave. The cost of the surgery was staggering—five hundred thousand pesos per eye. In total, I faced an expense of around one million pesos for the entire treatment. A lump formed in my throat as I processed the numbers. I felt a rush of frustration and despair wash over me.

I glanced at my bank account on my phone—eighty thousand pesos was all that remained. It felt like a cruel joke, a stark reminder of how quickly things could change. I had worked hard for my savings, and the thought of losing it all was unbearable. Where could I possibly turn for financial assistance? My mind raced with questions, each one heavier than the last.

Dr. Lim, noticing my distress, mentioned a charity option at Vicente Sotto Memorial Hospital, a government hospital in Cebu City. The idea of navigating a charity system felt daunting, but it was a glimmer of hope amidst the overwhelming darkness. As I left the hospital, the weight of the news pressed down on me, and I struggled to catch my breath.

When I finally arrived home safely at six in the evening, the world outside seemed to carry on as if nothing had changed. I walked straight into my room, the familiar surroundings offering little comfort. As I sat on the edge of my bed, tears streamed down my cheeks. The news felt too heavy to bear, and the sense of loss was palpable. I wished I were back in Dubai, surrounded by friends who could help lift my spirits. I longed for the carefree days when my biggest concern was where to find the best shawarma, not whether I would lose my sight or my career.

The anxiety gnawed at me—what if I couldn't afford the treatment? What if this was the end of my dreams, my ambitions? I was terrified of losing my savings and, even more, the career I had worked so hard to build. My mind spiraled into a dark place, filled with "what ifs" and fears of an uncertain future.

That night, as I sat in the dim light of my room, I felt the weight of uncertainty pressing down on me. The thought of losing my hard-earned funds was daunting, and I knew I had to take action. After much contemplation, I decided to approach my mother with an idea that had been forming in my mind: opening a mini grocery store right in front of our house. This venture could provide a steady income and help us sustain our daily expenses.With a clear vision in mind, I began to budget my remaining money carefully. I made a list of essential items we could sell—rice, canned goods, snacks, and basic household supplies. I envisioned the store as a hub for our neighborhood, a place where people could gather and find what they needed without traveling far.

In addition to the grocery store, I wanted to explore every possible avenue to secure our financial future. I planned to apply for a charity program at Vicente Sotto Memorial Hospital, seeking assistance as an overseas worker. I hoped that by tapping into these resources, I could pave a way toward stability for my family.

Furthermore, I looked into applying for financial assistance from the Overseas Workers Welfare Administration. I knew that the support they offered could be crucial in helping us navigate this financial crisis. I took a deep breath and reminded myself that I was capable of overcoming these challenges.I spent the next few days preparing my proposals and gathering the necessary documents. My mother supported my plans wholeheartedly, encouraging me every step of the way. We discussed the importance of perseverance and resilience in tough times, and I felt a renewed sense of determination.

In addition to my plans for the grocery store, I realized I needed to address the future of Jetliner Express, our travel agency, which I co-owned with Dennis, Aline, and Vera. After weighing my options, I decided to move the agency's operations to my home in Liloan. This change would eliminate the monthly rental fees that had been a significant strain on our budget, as well as the contract for one of our staff members. To ensure a smooth transition, I set up a dedicated office space in a corner of our living room. It felt invigorating to turn our home into a hub of activity. I retained Kenneth as my office assistant; he had always been reliable and understood the ins and outs of our business. With Kenneth by my side, I could manage the agency more closely, making it easier to cut costs and streamline our operations.

That same night, I reached out to Dennis, our finance manager, to share my plans. He was supportive and encouraged me to move forward. We discussed the logistics of relocating the agency, and he assured me that as long as the changes didn't negatively impact my health, he would back my operational strategies. Dennis also promised to cover the majority of our expenses during this transitional period, understanding that my budget was tight and I had no other work at that moment. His support lifted a weight off my shoulders, and I felt grateful to have partners who believed in our collective vision. With everyone on board, we started to map out how to run the agency effectively from home. We discussed how to maintain our client relationships and ensure that our services remained top-notch, even in this new setting. I felt a renewed sense of purpose as I envisioned the agency thriving despite the challenges we faced. As the days passed, we implemented our plans, balancing the demands of both the grocery store and the travel agency. It was no small feat, but with determination and teamwork, I knew we could navigate this challenging time together.

However, not every day was smooth sailing. Tough times struck when my parents decided to travel to the city. On their way home , they were involved in a collision with a firetruck in Consolacion. The front end of our car was completely wrecked, but thankfully, my parents emerged from the accident unharmed. Their safety was a relief, yet the emotional toll was heavy, especially for my mother, who felt the weight of despair as we grappled with the aftermath. After the incident, my parents promptly went to the police station to file a complaint against the firetruck driver. However, their hopes of getting compensation for the car repairs were dashed when they learned that the firetruck was government-owned. This complicated matters, leaving my parents feeling frustrated and helpless. As the reality of the situation sank in, my mother's sadness was palpable. I could see the strain in her eyes, and I felt a deep sense of responsibility to support her. I had bought my red car through a loan from BDO Unibank, and I had barely paid it off for less than a year. Upon reviewing the documents, I realized I had opted for only basic third-party insurance. This oversight meant that if I needed to repair the car, it would cost me around thirty thousand pesos—an amount that loomed large given my already precarious financial situation. The burden of this unexpected expense felt overwhelming. With my remaining funds dwindling, I struggled to figure out how I could cover the costs. I felt a wave of disappointment wash over me, not just because of the car's damage, but because I had worked so hard to create stability for my family. It was disheartening to see our efforts threatened by unforeseen circumstances.

I walked slowly toward my car, my heart heavy with emotion. As I approached the wreckage, tears streamed down my face. This car had been a gift to my father, a symbol of my love and gratitude for everything he had done for us. Now, seeing it damaged and battered felt like a crushing blow. With trembling hands, I gently placed my palm on the crumpled hood, as if trying to absorb the shock of what had happened. The reality of my situation weighed down on me—I was already struggling to meet my monthly obligations to the bank, and now this accident threatened to derail everything I had worked so hard for.

At that moment of despair, I found myself crying out to God for help. "Lord, what is happening to me? Lord, please help me!" My voice trembled as I poured out my heart, feeling both vulnerable and desperate. I had always believed in the power of prayer, but now, more than ever, I felt the need for reassurance and strength.

As I stood there, a mix of fear and sadness coursed through me. I thought about all the plans I had for my family, the grocery store, and the travel agency. It felt like everything was slipping through my fingers. Yet, even amidst the turmoil, I realized that I couldn't let this define my journey. I needed to find a way forward. Taking a deep breath, I wiped my tears and began to think of practical steps I could take. I reminded myself that challenges often come with lessons, and I had to keep my faith strong. Perhaps this was a moment to lean on my family and friends, to seek their support and guidance as we navigated this difficult time together.

As the days went by, I found it increasingly difficult to sleep. The weight of stress settled heavily on my shoulders, leaving me restless and exhausted. Each night was a battle against my racing thoughts, worries about my finances, and the uncertainty of our situation. I could hardly remember the last time I felt truly at ease.

Then, a ray of hope appeared when Sally, a friend and Aline's best friend, reached out to me with an inquiry about an upcoming tour to Hong Kong. She wanted to plan a trip for herself, her daughter, and her mother. I felt a surge of excitement at the prospect of creating a tailored itinerary for them. It was a chance not only to help them but also to reinvigorate my spirits.

After a series of negotiations, guided by Aline's impressive negotiating skills, we successfully closed the deal. I was thrilled to see the project take shape, knowing it would generate much-needed income. The earnings from that tour provided a significant financial boost, helping me cover some of the costs associated with my car repairs.

Once the profits were calculated and I distributed shares to Dennis and Aline, a sense of relief washed over me. It wasn't a complete solution to my financial challenges, but it was a step in the right direction. With each small victory, my confidence grew—I was learning to manage my obstacles and was determined to keep pushing forward, no matter what challenges lay ahead.

Despite the myriad challenges and my personal battles, I remained hopeful about pursuing my medical treatment. I made numerous trips to Vicente Sotto Memorial Hospital, waking up early each morning and returning home late in the evening, all in search of financial assistance and medical help from the government. Each visit was filled with a mix of hope and despair, but I was determined to persist. Sadly, after weeks of back-and-forth visits to the government hospital, I was informed that I wouldn't be receiving the medical treatment I needed due to a lack of medical equipment. They referred me back to the Eye Institute of Chong Hua Hospital, a facility known for its specialized care. While the news was disheartening, I held onto a glimmer of hope.

Photo Credit: Chong Hua Hospital,www.chonghua.com.ph

A few weeks later, I returned to Chong Hua Hospital and met with Dr. Lim again. I explained my situation and the urgency of my condition, asking for financial assistance. To my relief, the endorsement letter from Vicente Sotto played a crucial role in securing a significant discount for my surgery. The operation would cost seventy thousand pesos, but with the help of PhilHealth disability benefits, I only had to cover around twenty thousand pesos for one eye. It felt like a small miracle amid my struggles.

On March 2019, I had my first surgery. The procedure was scheduled to begin at one o'clock in the afternoon, and I felt a mix of anxiety and anticipation. The surgery lasted for five long hours, focusing on my right eye. I underwent a vitrectomy surgery , where a gas bubble was inserted to push my retina back into its proper position. As I lay on the operating table, the reality of the situation hit me. The sterile environment, the bright lights, and the team of medical professionals surrounding me only heightened my nerves. My heart raced, and I struggled to catch my breath. Dr. Lim asked me twice if I wanted to continue with the procedure, clearly sensing my fear. But deep down, I was resolute. I knew that this was my chance to regain my vision and see the world clearly again. I was determined to push through the pain and fear, fueled by the hope of a brighter future.

As the procedure began, I focused on that hope. I envisioned the everyday moments I longed to experience again—seeing my parents' smiles, the vibrant colors of nature, and the faces of my friends. I clung to that vision, knowing that enduring this pain was a step toward reclaiming my life. The hours passed slowly, each minute feeling like an eternity. But I held on, knowing that every moment was a part of my journey toward healing.

After the long hours of surgery, I felt utterly exhausted. The doctors advised me to rest at home for seven to fourteen days, emphasizing the importance of recovery. However, sleeping and eating proved to be difficult since I had to lay face down on my bed to allow the gas bubble to do its job. The days dragged on, but I began to notice a glimmer of improvement in my right eye as the gas bubble started to dissipate. Despite the doctor's warnings, I couldn't bear the thought of being idle any longer. I decided to stand up and help my parents manage our grocery store. One afternoon, while my parents went to our farm in Danao City, about thirty miles away, I was left alone in the store with my brother, Daniel. He was sixteen years old and had cerebral palsy, which meant he couldn't walk, stand, or eat by himself. It was a challenge, but one I faced with love and determination.

That day, my Auntie Liza visited us to help feed Daniel. To my surprise, I overheard them arguing. The harsh words they exchanged stung deeply as she cursed my brother for his condition. It broke my heart to see Daniel caught in the middle of such a conflict, a victim of circumstances beyond his control. Feeling the weight of the moment, I carefully lifted my brother and moved him to his chair. He was heavy, and the strain of carrying him sent an intense headache throbbing through the right side of my head. Once I settled him in, I made my way to our agency, hoping to find a quiet moment to rest on the couch. As I sat down, I noticed something unsettling: a dark spot appeared in the upper corner of my vision, like a splash of black ink on a pristine white cloth. Panic gripped me as my hands began to shake and my breath quickened. I felt a sense of dread wash over me. Kenneth, my trusted office assistant, came in and noticed my distress. He quickly guided me to my room, urging me to take a break. But as the hours passed, my vision began to fade to grey. I could no longer see any objects in my surroundings clearly; everything morphed into a blur of shapes and shadows.

In that moment, fear overwhelmed me. I had fought so hard to regain my sight, and now it felt like I was slipping away from that hard-earned victory. I couldn't help but wonder if I was facing yet another setback, and I desperately hoped for clarity, both in my vision and in my life.

When my parents returned home, they quickly discovered what had transpired. My father was furious with Auntie Liza, and the tension in the air was palpable. Auntie Liza lived on the other side of our house; she was an old maid, alone and without children. Her strict and sometimes insensitive demeanor often led to conflicts within our family. In the heat of the moment, to restore some peace, she was forced to leave our home and rent a nearby apartment. I felt a deep sense of sadness at the rift that had formed between my father and my aunt. Family conflicts were never easy, and the weight of it all added to my emotional burden. Yet, despite the chaos around me, my primary focus was on seeking assistance from Dr. Lim, the surgeon who had operated on my right eye.

The next day, we returned to the Eye Institute. I felt a mixture of hope and anxiety as we waited to see Dr. Lim. When I finally spoke with him, the news was disheartening. He informed me that my retina had detached again, and I would need to undergo another surgery. This time, the gas bubble would be replaced with silicone oil to stabilize the retina. To make matters worse, Dr. Lim explained that cataracts were also affecting the outer layer of my lenses in both eyes. He suggested a combined surgery for my retina and cataract, presenting me with a quotation for the procedures. The total cost was seventy thousand pesos, a staggering amount that felt like a heavy weight on my already burdened heart.

As I left the clinic, sadness enveloped me. I returned home and retreated to my room, refusing to take dinner. I felt an overwhelming anger toward myself for not paying closer attention to my medical situation earlier. The reality of my circumstances sank in, and I couldn't shake the feeling of regret. I had fought so hard to regain my sight, yet here I was, facing yet another setback.In the stillness of my room, I struggled with my emotions. I reflected on my journey—the hope I had felt, the determination I had shown, and now, the crushing disappointment.

The cost of cataract surgery can be staggering, especially when factoring in the type of artificial lens used. In my case, I faced a difficult choice: the expensive U.S.-made lenses or the more affordable Indian-made ones, which were roughly priced at 40,000 pesos per lensis—not including the surgeon's fees or hospital bills. The financial burden was overwhelming, and I found myself feeling desperate for help.

After much hesitation, I reached out to my best friend, Dennis. I explained my situation, pouring out my fears and worries. To my relief, he agreed to help finance my surgery. Days passed, and soon Dennis arrived in Cebu after taking a short vacation in his hometown of Capiz. His presence brought me a sense of comfort and reassurance that I desperately needed. On the day of the surgery, my mother and Dennis accompanied me to the Eye Institute. As we sat in the waiting lounge, I could feel their unwavering support enveloping me like a warm blanket. Despite the anxiety swirling in my mind, their presence calmed my nerves.

When my name was finally called, I was led into the operating room. The bright lights and sterile smell heightened my apprehension. The surgery lasted nearly six hours. As the procedure progressed, I experienced a level of pain that felt unbearable. I struggled to keep my composure, doubting whether I could endure it all. At that moment, I wanted nothing more than to wake up from this nightmare.

After the surgery, exhaustion washed over me. I felt drained, both physically and emotionally. My mother and Dennis were there, their faces etched with concern. I could sense their sincerity, their worry for my well-being, and it broke my heart. Doctor Lim approached us with a solemn expression. He informed us that the surgery had been successful, but he couldn't guarantee a positive prognosis due to the severe damage to my retina. His words hung heavy in the air, amplifying my fears. He emphasized the power of prayer, suggesting that faith could play a crucial role in my healing. At that moment, I was struck by the gravity of my situation. The uncertainty about my vision felt overwhelming. I struggled to process everything—the pain, the fear, and the potential outcomes. But amid this turmoil, I clung to the hope that the surgery might still bring some light back into my life. As the days turned into weeks, I began my recovery. Each morning was a new challenge, filled with both physical discomfort and the emotional weight of what lay ahead. Yet, my mother and Dennis remained by my side, offering encouragement and companionship. They would sit with me for hours, sharing stories and laughter, reminding me that I was not alone in this battle.

After the surgery, Dennis booked a nearby hotel for us so we could rest without the long journey back to Liloan, which would take over an hour. As I lay in bed, exhaustion washing over me, I could hear the soft murmur of Dennis and my mother praying for my recovery. Their voices were filled with concern, and I could hear my mother quietly crying, her emotions palpable in the small hotel room. It was a moment steeped in love and worry, one that deepened my resolve to heal.

The next day, my father, my brother Daniel ,and Kenneth, came to pick us up from the hotel. We decided to head straight to a restaurant in SM Mall of Consolacion for lunch. The bustling atmosphere was a welcome distraction from the heaviness that had surrounded us. Everyone was hungry, and as we settled around the table, laughter began to replace the earlier sadness. To lighten the mood further, Dennis suggested we take a quick vacation to Bantayan Island. The idea of a change of scenery felt refreshing. After lunch, while the rest of the family prepared our things for the trip, I took a moment to rest in my room, letting the thought of the island wash over me. I imagined the soft, white sands and the gentle sound of the waves lapping at the shore. Even in my fragile state, the thought of being surrounded by beauty and tranquility ignited a spark of hope within me. I knew this brief escape would not only help lift my spirits but also allow me to reconnect with my family in a joyful setting.

As they packed, I could hear their excitement. They were determined to make this trip a bright spot in the midst of my recovery. With each passing moment, I felt the warmth of their support wrapping around me like a comforting embrace, giving me strength as I prepared to face the days ahead.

We departed early in the morning, eager for the adventure ahead. After a three-hour drive from my hometown, we finally reached the Hagnaya port. There were seven of us in the mini-van: my father at the wheel, me beside him, my younger brother Daniel, Kenneth—my loyal assistant, my uncle

Artemio-who is my mother's older brother, my mother, and Dennis. Along for the ride were my two beloved Chihuahua dogs, Cosey and Cokey. They were more than just pets; they had been my companions since 2013

when I was working as a manager in Makati City. Their presence always brought me joy and comfort. As we boarded the ferry to Bantayan Island, excitement buzzed in the air. The salty sea breeze swept through the deck, filling us with a sense of freedom and anticipation. I watched the waves churn beneath us, the sunlight sparkling on the water like a thousand tiny diamonds. Cosey and Cokey, nestled comfortably in Dennis and in my arm seemed to sense the excitement too, their little tails wagging furiously. The atmosphere was light and cheerful, a stark contrast to the heaviness I had felt just days before. As the ferry began to move, I could see my family laughing and chatting, their spirits lifted by the promise of a beautiful getaway. Dennis leaned over to me and said, "This is exactly what you need. A little sun and sea will do wonders for your recovery." I smiled, grateful for his unwavering support.

The journey across the water felt refreshing, the gentle rocking of the ferry calming my mind. With each passing moment, I felt more and more at ease. Bantayan Island was just ahead, a paradise waiting to be explored, and I couldn't wait to soak in its beauty and create new memories with my loved ones. We spent two wonderful days on Bantayan Island, each filled with joy and laughter. The sun warmed our skin, and the sound of the waves created a soothing backdrop to our time together. We explored the island, indulged in delicious seafood, and shared stories as we lounged on the beach. For those two days, I was able to forget my worries and simply enjoy the moment. But as all good things must, our quick vacation came to an end. Dennis had to leave to fly back to Dubai for work, and as we gathered for our goodbyes, a sense of unease crept in.

"I wish I had normal eyesight so I could come back to Dubai and continue my career," I admitted, feeling a wave of insecurity wash over me. It was hard not to think about the uncertainty of my condition and how it might affect my future. In June of that same year, I received a message from Aline, and my heart skipped a beat. She wanted to visit me with her family! It seemed she had missed me immensely and wanted to celebrate her older brother's birthday with us. I was filled with excitement and delight at the thought of seeing them again. Just a few days later, Aline and her entire family arrived in Liloan.

They brought with them her sister Shelo, her older brother—the birthday celebrant, his wife, Kyle-her niece, and Kyle's husband, along with Dylan, her adorable grandson. Most importantly, Aline's loving mother was there too.

The warmth of their presence filled our home with joy. When Aline embraced me, I felt an outpouring of sincerity and concern. It was a comforting reminder of the bonds we shared. She handed me a special gift: a miniature aircraft she had bought from Cebu Pacific. The thoughtful gesture brought a huge smile to my face, and at that moment, I felt a surge of happiness.

They stayed at our house for a few days, and during their visit, we celebrated her brother's birthday with laughter, good food, and joyful memories. The atmosphere was vibrant, filled with stories and the sounds of happiness echoing throughout our home. We also took a quick trip to our farm in Danao City. I cherished the smiles on Aline's mother's face as she explored the greenery and enjoyed the fresh air. She expressed her desire to visit us again, and I felt a warm glow inside knowing how much she appreciated our time together. As we gathered for meals and shared moments, it became clear that this visit was about more than just a birthday celebration; it was a testament to the enduring friendships and love that bind us, no matter the distance. I felt grateful for these connections, especially during a time when I needed them most.

After Aline and her family returned from their vacation in my hometown, I found myself grappling with the same insecurities that had crept in when Dennis left for Dubai. The warmth of their visit faded, and I was left with a sense of longing. I wished more than anything for a clear vision, a chance to regain my independence, and the opportunity to work again and pursue my dreams in Canada.

Every night, I lay awake, wishing it was all just a bad dream—this uncertainty and fear surrounding my eyesight. I yearned for a fairy godmother to appear and wave her magic wand, restoring my sight and bringing back the carefree days when I felt whole and capable. The thought of returning to a life filled with possibility was comforting, yet it felt so far out of reach. I couldn't shake the feeling of being trapped in my current situation, yearning for the life I had imagined for myself. Each passing day felt like a reminder of what I was missing, and I struggled to find hope amid the shadows of my insecurities. As I reflected on the love and support from my friends and family, I tried to hold onto that glimmer of hope. Perhaps, with time and perseverance, I could overcome these challenges and find my way back to my dreams. But for now, the weight of my fears lingered, and I continued to wish for a little magic to guide me through.

A few weeks later, my mother and I decided to invest in another business, this time focusing on health and wellness. It involved leverage marketing, or networking, which promised great returns on investment. Encouraged by the potential, my mother made the bold decision to submit her land title to apply for a mortgage, hoping to secure the necessary funds to kickstart our venture. As we launched our business, we began receiving bulk orders of various health products. It was exhilarating to see our hard work pay off as we connected with clients and built our network. We organized orientation sessions and seminars for prospective clients, sharing the benefits of our products and the business model we believed in.

I took on an active role, even stepping into the spotlight as a speaker. Conducting a series of training sessions for our new members was both challenging and rewarding. I enjoyed sharing my knowledge and inspiring others to take charge of their health and financial futures. The camaraderie among our team was palpable, and I felt a renewed sense of purpose. Everything seemed to be falling into place. The operations ran smoothly, and we were gaining traction in the market. My mother and I worked long hours, but the satisfaction of building something together brought us closer. We could see our efforts blossoming, and it felt like a new chapter was unfolding, full of promise and potential.

I had the opportunity to meet the owners and board members of the company, Jstore, and it felt like a turning point in my life. The company opened a new chapter for me, and

I became increasingly busy, focusing on its operations to gain clients and boost sales. The excitement of being part of something larger fueled my determination. In my enthusiasm, I encouraged my friends, including Dennis, to invest in this venture as well. He decided to invest a substantial amount, around a hundred thousand pesos, believing in the potential of the business. It felt rewarding to share this journey with those I cared about, and I hoped it would lead to collective success. As I immersed myself in this new role, I set my mind on forging ahead, not just as a networker but as someone who could create meaningful opportunities for myself and others. The prospect of building a life there motivated me to work even harder.

Each day brought new challenges and victories, and I embraced them all. The connections I was making and the skills I was developing were invaluable. I felt a renewed sense of purpose and direction, and with each milestone we reached, I grew more confident in my ability to shape my future. The journey ahead was still uncertain, but for the first time in a while, I felt hopeful. I was ready to take on the world, one step at a time, believing that this was just the beginning of something great. While I was focusing on my venture, I was also preparing for my third eye operation. I returned to Chong Hua Hospital Eye Institute for the next series of steps concerning my left eye. Dr. Lim suggested using silicone oil instead of a gas bubble this time, expressing uncertainty about the results if we continued with the gas bubble approach. He also recommended combining the cataract operation with a vitrectomy surgery.

At that moment, I felt a sense of clarity and determination. I had faith in Dr. Lim's expertise and was ready to pursue his recommendations. I scheduled my left eye operation for February 2020, feeling a mix of hope and anxiety. The surgery took about three hours, much quicker than the operation on my right eye. I remember feeling a wave of relief as I was wheeled into the operating room, confident that I was taking a significant step toward regaining my vision. I followed every instruction from Dr. Lim meticulously, eager to ensure the best possible outcome.

In the days following the surgery, I made sure to use the health products from my business, believing that they would support my recovery. With each passing day, I held onto hope, envisioning a future where I could see clearly again—a future that included both my growing business and the dreams I had for my life in Canada. This journey had been fraught with challenges, but I was determined to face whatever came next with resilience and optimism.

On March 12, 2020, I celebrated my 36th birthday in a way I would never forget. My sister Caryl, along with some of my office staff members, had organized a surprise birthday party for me. They transformed a space inside our compound into a vibrant celebration, adorned with colorful balloons and a delicious spread of different foods. As I walked in, I was overwhelmed with joy and gratitude. The warmth of their smiles and heartfelt greetings enveloped me, making me feel incredibly loved. When it came time to blow out the candles on my birthday cake, I paused for a moment, reflecting on the journey that had brought me to this point. Memories of my 34th birthday in Dubai flooded my mind—a time filled with excitement and new beginnings.The laughter, the food, and the love shared that day became a beautiful reminder that life, despite its uncertainties, could still be filled with joy and connection. It was a birthday I would cherish forever, marking not just another year, but a renewed commitment to embrace every opportunity life had to offer.

Just a few minutes later, my phone rang. It was Ivanmarc, a good friend of mine from college who was working in Malacañang Palace. He called with urgent news that sent a wave of concern through me. The president of the Philippines and his cabinet members were planning to close the borders as soon as possible due to the rapid spread of COVID-19. At that moment, my heart raced. My brother-in-law Jeff was in Manila, and we were all deeply worried about how the planned border closure would affect him. It felt like the ground beneath us was shifting, and the gravity of the situation hit hard. With heavy hearts, we had to cut our celebration short. Instead of continuing the festivities, we rushed back to the office to issue a ticket for Jeff's return to Cebu. As we worked to prepare all the necessary documentation for our clients and upcoming tour projects, an air of anxiety hung over us. The uncertainty of the situation was palpable; we were scared of what would happen next and how this unprecedented event would impact our lives and businesses. The joyous atmosphere of my birthday celebration had quickly transformed into a whirlwind of worry and urgency. As we made calls and coordinated logistics, I couldn't help but reflect on how quickly things could change. The world felt like it was turning upside down, and I braced myself for the challenges that lay ahead.

On March 18, the national government implemented a sweeping closure of all provincial and regional borders, mandating that everyone stay at home. Our businesses had to stop operating, and I initially thought this would last only a week or two, maybe even a month. However, as time went on, the reality of the COVID-19 pandemic became increasingly serious. The virus spread rapidly throughout the Philippines and the world, resulting in countless lives lost.

The impact on our operations was devastating. We had to cancel one of our biggest projects at Jetliner Express, which was set to bring 300 Chinese tourists to the Philippines for a 15-day tour. This was a significant loss, not just financially but also in terms of the dreams and aspirations we had built around that project. Many of our other upcoming tours were also affected, leading to a cascade of cancellations that left us reeling. As a travel agency, we had to quickly adapt to the new reality. Our operations shifted to flexible working hours, with most of our team working remotely from home. This adjustment was far from easy. We faced numerous challenges, including limited resources, outdated technology, and unstable internet connections, all of which added to our burdens. With each passing week, we started to feel the financial strain. Income dwindled as travel ground to a halt, and I watched helplessly as Jetliner Express, the company I had managed for years, had to cease operations. The weight of uncertainty loomed heavily over us, and I felt a mix of frustration and sadness as I faced the reality of our situation. It was a trying time, filled with difficult decisions and emotional turmoil. But amidst the chaos, I held onto the hope that we could weather this storm and emerge stronger on the other side.

Our grocery store and my mother's guesthouse had to close quickly, mirroring the fate of Jetliner Express. The Jstore networking business also faced a temporary shutdown, and we found ourselves unable to withdraw our investments. It felt like a perfect storm of challenges, and we were caught in the middle, facing both financial and emotional drain. The limited support from the government barely alleviated our struggles. We often had to line up for hours just to receive a small bag of groceries, enough to meet our daily needs but hardly sufficient to cover our family's requirements. Each trip felt like a reminder of the reality we were facing, and it was disheartening to see how many others

where in the same situation. It became increasingly difficult for me to spend even a little money on my medication, as I needed to save every penny for the days ahead. The stress of financial uncertainty weighed heavily on my shoulders, and I could feel my resilience being tested.

To compound these challenges, my vision began to deteriorate. I started seeing clouds in my eyes, making it hard to focus on objects close to me. Each day felt like a reminder of the battles I was fighting, both physically and emotionally. The fear of losing my sight intensified, and I couldn't help but feel overwhelmed by the combination of financial hardship and deteriorating health. As I navigated this difficult period, I tried to hold onto hope, clinging to the belief that we would eventually overcome these trials. But each setback felt like another layer of weight pressing down on me.

It took months before the government partially eased the border restrictions, and we slowly began to reopen Jetliner Express. However, we quickly noticed the profound changes in the travel landscape; all of our tour projects that had once seemed promising were now gone. Fear had gripped everyone, and the desire to travel had all but vanished. At that moment, I found myself losing faith in the future of our business. To make matters worse, Ed, one of our business partners, decided to withdraw her partnership with us. This decision brought significant losses and left us reeling, both

financially and emotionally. Dennis and I knew we had to strategize carefully to sustain the business, but every avenue we explored felt daunting. The marketing landscape seemed almost impossible to navigate under the current circumstances, and despite our best efforts, we struggled to regain the trust of our previous customers. Our networking business was also facing a steep decline in sales. With fewer people willing to invest in health products during such uncertain times, our inventory began to pile up in storage. We grew increasingly worried as we realized that some of our products were approaching their expiration dates. The thought of losing not just our investments but also the livelihoods we had built was a heavy burden to bear. Each day felt like a battle against the odds, and I often found myself questioning how we would pull through. Despite the setbacks, Dennis and I remained committed to finding solutions. We brainstormed ideas and explored new marketing strategies, but the road ahead felt incredibly challenging.

The weight of the uncertainties and heavy trials I was facing began to take a toll on my emotional well-being. I became increasingly temperamental, easily angered by the smallest things, and I found myself shouting at the people around me. Decisions that I once approached with patience now felt overwhelming, and I terminated several employees over minor issues, a choice I later regretted. Tensions ran high within my family as well. There were instances when my sister and her husband and I had heated arguments, each conflict fueled by the stress we were all experiencing. Worst of all, I reached a breaking point and shouted at my mother—an act that felt completely out of character for me. In those moments, I felt like I was losing control, behaving in ways that I couldn't understand.

I was engulfed by a confusion and disorder of emotions: anxiety, sadness, and an anger that seemed to surface from nowhere. The weight of depression loomed large, and I struggled to process my feelings. I knew that my reactions were a reflection of the turmoil within me, but understanding it was another matter entirely. The isolation and fear of the pandemic only exacerbated these feelings. I felt trapped in a cycle of negativity, where each day blurred into the next, and I struggled to find a way to break free. I longed for a sense of peace and clarity, but instead, I was mired in confusion and frustration. It became clear that I needed to seek help and find healthier ways to cope with the challenges that surrounded me, but I found nothing.

One day, three of my friends from my previous job came to visit me after hearing about my situation. When they arrived, I could see the shock on their faces. They remembered me as the lively, joyful person I had been back in 2008, full of energy and optimism. But now, they could feel the sadness that had enveloped me, along with noticeable changes in my physical appearance. During their visits, we reminisced about the good old days, sharing laughter and stories from our youth. For a brief moment, it felt like a return to happier times, and I thought we were reconnecting. However, that sense of joy was short-lived. After two visits, they suddenly stopped coming, leaving me confused and hurt. It wasn't until I spoke with Theresa, one of our mutual friends, that I learned the truth. She revealed that my so-called close friends didn't want to visit me anymore because they found it too painful to see me in my current state.

They felt a heaviness in their hearts while looking at me and talking with me, and it lingered long after they left my home in Liloan. Rather than face that discomfort, they chose to distance themselves from me, believing it was easier to avoid the pain than to confront it.This revelation stung deeply. I couldn't understand how the friends I had once shared so much with could turn away during my time of need. The loneliness of my situation intensified, and I felt abandoned at a moment when I needed support the most. I longed for genuine connection and understanding, but instead, I was left grappling with the reality that some people couldn't bear to witness my struggles. It was a painful reminder of how isolating this journey had become, even among those I once considered close.

There are times when I find myself longing for the company of my nephews and niece, as well as the warmth that my older sister brings. They only visit us for special occasions—birthdays, holidays, and family gatherings. Most days, however, our house feels empty, echoing with silence as we wait for them to come and acknowledge our existence. It's during these quiet moments that I often reflect on the nature of our relationships. All of my nephews and niece are now in their teenage years, navigating the complexities of growing up. They're busy with their personal errands, household chores, online classes, and modular learning. I understand that they have their own lives to manage, but sometimes it feels as if they've drifted too far away. They seem like different people, living in a world that I no longer fully connect with.

The gap between us grows wider, and I can't help but feel a sense of loss. I often envy the families I see around me—those who have strong bonds with one another, where parents and siblings share laughter, support, and love. I watch as they gather around dining tables, engage in playful banter, and celebrate each other's achievements. In contrast, my family feels distant, as if we are merely passing ships in the night.

The realization that we have to beg for their attention just to have them visit weighs heavily on my heart. It's as if our love is conditional, tied to the occasions rather than the everyday moments that truly matter.

To bridge this growing gap, I took the initiative to offer my skills as a tutor. I thought that by helping them with their studies, we might rebuild some of the connection we once had. To my relief, they agreed, and I could see a flicker of happiness in their eyes. Our tutoring sessions became a small beacon of hope, allowing us to share laughter, frustrations, and even the occasional bonding moment over difficult math problems or challenging essays. Yet, despite these efforts, I still yearn for more. I want to create lasting memories, to be a part of their lives beyond just the role of a tutor. I dream of weekends filled with laughter, movie nights, and spontaneous adventures that would strengthen our bond. But I often wonder if they feel the same way or if they are too caught up in their own worlds to notice. As I reflect on these feelings, I remind myself that relationships take time and effort.

I thought that I had reached the lowest point of my painful situation, but a few weeks later, I received a call from my aunt in England, Auntie Leony, my mother's elder sister. I had hoped she was just checking in on us, but instead, her call turned into an unexpected and painful confrontation. Through Messenger, she began to nag me, unleashing a barrage of negative comments about my character and my disabilities. The most hurtful words echoed in my mind long after our conversation ended: "Why are you still trying to sustain your business? You're already blind, and who will help you? You're just a burden to your parents."

At that moment, I felt utterly lost. The weight of her words crashed down on me like a tidal wave, leaving me feeling devastated and deeply discriminated against because of my disabilities. I had already been grappling with my own fears and insecurities, and now I felt as if someone was reinforcing the worst of those thoughts. After our conversation, I retreated to my room and cried all night. Each tear was a release of the pent-up frustration, sadness, and anger that had been building inside me. I began to hate the world, the people around me, and, most painfully, myself. I felt abandoned by those I had once relied on for support, and the isolation I experienced was suffocating.

In that dark hour, even my faith in God felt distant. I questioned everything—the purpose of my struggles, the worth of my existence, and the dreams I had once held close. It was a moment of profound despair, one that left me feeling like I was sinking into an abyss, with no way out. That conversation with Aunt Leony triggered an overwhelming wave of pain and anxiety that left me unable to sleep for a few nights. I felt restless and exhausted, my mind spiraling through a labyrinth of painful memories and harsh realities. The emotional toll was relentless, and I found myself trapped in a cycle of negative thoughts that felt inescapable. To make matters worse, whenever I turned on the television or opened YouTube on my phone, I was bombarded with grim news about the increasing death toll due to COVID-19. The headlines seemed to scream at me, amplifying my anxiety. "Is this the end of the world? Why does it feel like everyone is terrified?" I questioned silently as I listened, feeling the weight of despair settle heavily on my chest. In my darkest moments, I found myself reflecting on the suffering all around us. I thought, "At least they are no longer in pain. At least they can no longer feel the anguish caused by earthly troubles." It was a morbid thought, but it stemmed from my own struggles and frustrations. The world felt so bleak, and I grappled with feelings of hopelessness, questioning the very fabric of life and the suffering we endure.

CHAPTER 5

AWAKENING

As I lay on my bed, the silence around me felt suffocating, amplifying the emptiness and loneliness that had settled deep within my soul. Even though my parents were under the same roof, there was a disconnect in our emotions that left me feeling more isolated than ever. We shared the space, but it felt as if we were worlds apart, each of us grappling with our own struggles in silence. I had friends, but one by one, they seemed to drift away, leaving me feeling abandoned in my time of need. My businesses, once a source of pride and purpose, were now faltering, closing down one after another. And while I had family and relatives, the support I craved felt like a distant dream, making me question the bonds that were supposed to hold us together. In moments of deep reflection, I found myself asking, "What is my purpose on Earth now that I'm blind and disabled?" The question echoed in my mind, a haunting reminder of my perceived limitations. I yearned for love and acceptance, but doubt crept in, making me wonder who would love me for who I truly am, in my current state of vulnerability. The weight of these thoughts was overwhelming. I felt lost in a world that seemed to offer no answers, no clarity. It was as if I were standing at the edge of a precipice, staring into an abyss of uncertainty.

It was precisely midnight of October 2021, my head ached fiercely, a persistent throb that refused to subside, intensifying with every flash of lightning that illuminated the night. The flickering light revealed fleeting shadows in my room, casting an eerie glow that heightened my sense of loneliness. With every rumble of thunder, memories flooded my mind—moments of laughter, love, and warmth that felt like distant dreams now. The rain outside seemed to echo my emotions, each drop a tear falling from my weary soul. I longed for a way out, for a glimmer of hope to pierce through the gloom that surrounded me. But instead, I felt trapped in this cycle of darkness, unable to escape the shadows that loomed large in my mind.

Two hours later, the heavy rains stopped and my room fell into darkness and silence. In this moment, unwelcome voices began to emerge from the shadows of my mind, whispering cruelly that I was worthless. They twisted around me like vines, suffocating any flicker of hope that had dared to linger. I fought against these thoughts, desperate to drown them out, yet they persisted, wearing down at my self-worth and fueling my sense of isolation.

As the weight of the silence pressed down on me, I realized that this internal battle was just as fierce as the storm that had raged outside. I felt trapped in a cycle of despair, where the absence of noise only heightened my insecurities. The quiet, once a welcome reprieve, now felt like an echo chamber for my darkest fears. All I could do was breathe and hope that somehow, I would find the strength to silence those voices, to reclaim my sense of self amidst the chaos within.

I stood up from my bed, a suffocating weight of despair pressing down on me. At that moment, it felt as if my 36 years of existence were utterly devoid of value. I contemplated ending it all, thinking about drinking insecticides or any poisonous liquid that could swiftly erase my pain. The idea wrapped around me like a dark shroud, promising an escape from the relentless suffering that had become my daily reality.

The voices in my mind grew louder, each one more damning than the last: "You're useless! You're a burden to your parents! Your life is worthless!" They echoed mercilessly, amplifying my feelings of isolation and hopelessness. Memories of dreams deferred and opportunities lost surged forward, reminding me of the weight of my failures. "I don't wanna leave, I wanna die"

My room was on the second floor, a space that once felt safe but now felt like a prison. As I opened the door, an overwhelming wave of emotion surged through me, and tears began to spill down my cheeks. My deepest sadness, anxiety, and depression crashed over me like a relentless tide, pushing me toward the thought of ending my life.

Each step down the staircase was heavy, weighted with the cruel reminders of my worthlessness. "You're a burden to everyone around you," the voices in my head echoed, each word reverberating in the hollow silence. The stairs felt like an obstacle course of despair, each step a painful reminder of my isolation and the chasm that seemed to widen between me and the world outside.

I gripped the banister, knuckles turning white, fighting against the urge to let go. My heart raced as I descended, torn between the suffocating pull of hopelessness and the faint glimmer of hope that flickered within me. Could I find a way back? The tears that fell were not just an expression of sorrow; they were a plea, a silent cry for understanding in a world that felt so unforgiving.

As I reached the bottom of the stairs, I felt an intense anger bubbling inside me—anger toward myself and toward the God who created me. "Why me?" I thought, grappling with the sheer unfairness of my situation. In the depths of my heart, I knew I had always prided myself on being a good person, a devoted servant, and a loving child. I wasn't a drug addict, a gambler, or a murderer. I followed the rules and respected the law, striving to live my life with integrity and purpose.

Yet, despite my efforts to do right, life had thrown me into a pit of despair that felt utterly undeserved. I watched as others who seemed to embrace chaos and disregard the rules led seemingly happy lives, while I struggled under the weight of my own sorrow. The stark contrast made my anger flare even more intensely. Why was I the one left to suffer? How could a higher power allow someone like me—someone who tried so hard to do everything right—to endure such relentless pain and turmoil?

As those questions churned in my mind, I felt a tempest of confusion and resentment brewing within me. The frustration gnawed at my insides, leading me to question everything: my faith, my choices, and the very fabric of my existence. I wanted answers—clarity and a reason for the suffering that seemed so unjust. It was as if my life had become a cruel joke, a series of unfortunate events that mocked my efforts to be virtuous.

The anger morphed into a heavy weight on my chest, pressing down on me with every breath. I wanted to shout to the universe. "Why does it feel like I'm being punished?" Each day felt like a battle against the darkness, and I found myself spiraling deeper into despair.

I walked toward the kitchen, enveloped in darkness and despair, when I noticed my father quietly preparing something. "What are you doing up, Pa? It's still three o'clock in the morning," I asked, my voice heavy with fatigue. He turned to me and explained that he was making milk for my mother. "Your mother is in pain; her head is aching and she can't sleep well."

My heart sank at the thought of her suffering. My mother was a cancer survivor, but the battle had left her body weak and vulnerable. I quickly made my way to their room at the ground floor , and as I entered, I saw her lying there, discomfort etched across her face. Without hesitation, I sat beside her and began to massage her head and shoulders, trying to offer some relief.

As I focused on my mother, a wave of realization washed over me. I felt so selfish. Here was a woman who had fought fiercely for her life, who had supported me through every ambition and plan I had ever dreamed of. People all around the world were battling their own struggles, doing their best to hold on to life, while I was entertaining thoughts of giving up.

At that moment, I understood that my mother was a fighter. She had endured so much, and yet here she was, still holding on. It struck me how easy it had become for me to dwell on my own pain, to think of surrendering when I had a family that relied on me. The weight of my despair felt lighter as I recognized the strength and resilience in my mother.

I realized that leaving them behind would be an act of selfishness, a choice that would inflict even more pain on those I loved. My mother had been my rock, and her unwavering support had carried me through the darkest times. I needed to honor her fight and find the strength within myself to keep going. In that quiet moment, surrounded by the warmth of my parents, I felt a flicker of hope—a reminder that perhaps there was still a reason to hold on.

After a few minutes, my mother finally fell asleep, and I walked back to my room, feeling the weight of the world on my shoulders. As I stepped slowly toward the edge of my bed, the tears began to fall. Guilt and pain overwhelmed me, and I couldn't hold back any longer. I cried hard, each sob echoing the turmoil inside me. In my anguish, I found myself pleading with God once again. "Why are you doing this to us? Why do I have to suffer like this? Are you even real?" It felt as if my heart was a candle, flickering and on the verge of losing its light and strength. I sank to my knees, feeling the cool floor beneath me, and cried out loud, "If you are real, show me right now! Show me your power! Prove to me that you are the God of the universe!"

At that moment, my words felt like a test—a desperate challenge born from the depths of my suffering. I was filled with a longing for answers, for a sign that I wasn't alone in this struggle. I needed reassurance that someone, somewhere, was listening to my cries and that there was meaning behind the pain I was enduring. As the tears continued to flow, I poured out my heart, hoping for a response, a flicker of hope in the darkness. I felt vulnerable yet determined, ready to confront whatever lay ahead. Would my faith be rewarded? Would I find the strength to keep going, or would I remain lost in this sea of despair?

As time passed, I eventually fell asleep on the cold floor, the weight of my emotions finally giving way to exhaustion. I was stirred awake by the sound of birds singing outside my window and the familiar footsteps of my father as he cleaned the ground outside the house. It was five-thirty in the morning when I realized I had fallen asleep on the floor. I stood up, hoping that everything that had transpired the night before had been nothing more than a nightmare.

But as I looked around, the emptiness and loneliness washed over me once again. The anxiety, frustration, sadness, and the heavy cloak of depression still clung to me, refusing to fade away. I felt like I was suffocating, yearning for a breath of fresh air. So, I decided to leave my room and step out towards our main door.

Our main door was a sliding glass door, and as I stepped down to our patio, a branch from the yellow bell plant brushed against my face, startling me for a moment. The vibrant color of the flowers stood in stark contrast to my mood, their brightness almost mocking my sorrow. I took a deep breath, trying to ground myself in the present, feeling the cool morning air wrap around me like a gentle embrace. As I stood there, I contemplated the new day ahead. Would it bring change? Would it be any different from the last?

The weight of uncertainty hung heavy in the air, but a small part of me held onto the hope that maybe, just maybe, today would offer a glimpse of light. For the past month and even the past year, I had failed to recognize the beauty of the yellow bell plant. This morning, however, felt different. It was as if I was seeing it for the first time, stunned by its vibrant color, which seemed to radiate warmth and life. Despite my blurry vision, which usually allowed me to see only ten to fifteen percent of the world around me, at that moment, everything became clear. I felt as though I had stepped into a different realm, one where colors were more vivid and life was more palpable. The bright yellow blooms stood out against the backdrop of the green foliage, their petals dancing in the gentle morning breeze.

At that fleeting moment of clarity, I marveled at the beauty that had always been there but had gone unnoticed. The yellow bells, with their cheerful hue, seemed to beckon me, reminding me that even in the midst of my struggles, there were still moments of beauty waiting to be discovered. It was a small yet profound revelation, awakening a sense of hope within me. As I stood there, captivated by the blossoms, I realized that perhaps I could learn to appreciate the small things again—those fleeting moments of joy that could break through the darkness. Maybe this was the beginning of a new perspective, one where I could find light in the shadows.

A few minutes later, as I continued to admire the beautiful yellow bells, the sun began to rise over the horizon. I noticed the golden light breaking through the dark nimbus clouds, casting a warm glow across everything around me. It was a beautiful sight, a reminder that even after the darkest storms, light would always return. As I turned back to close the sliding glass door, something caught my eye. I saw an image reflected in the glass. Technically, it was me, but the figure that stared back felt different.

Standing before me, illuminated by the sun's radiant light, was a man whose face I could not quite recognize. Yet deep within, I knew who He was—Jesus Christ. A shiver ran down my spine, and I felt goosebumps erupted all over my body. At that moment, all my doubts and questions flooded back to me. I remembered the words I had spoken in anger, my phrases testing His existence and power. But now, in His presence, everything has changed. I felt His grace enveloping me like a warm embrace.

I sensed His existence around me and His power surging within me, transforming my pain into hope. A wave of disbelief washed over me. Was this real, or was I dreaming?

I questioned my own perception, my heart racing with the enormity of what I had experienced. At that fleeting moment, the weight of my struggles seemed to lift, replaced by a profound sense of peace and assurance. As I stood there, grappling with my emotions, I realized that this encounter might be the turning point I had longed for—a moment of divine connection that could guide me through the darkness.

After that encounter, I felt a newfound sense of clarity and warmth within me. I walked toward my father, who was diligently cleaning our grounds and arranging the plants in the garden. As I approached him, I hesitated for a moment, then reached out and took hold of his right shoulder. For the first time in a long while, I greeted him with a smile that felt genuine and bright. Since childhood, my relationship with my father has been strained.

He was a strict man, a good provider, but our time together was limited; as a former overseas worker, he was only home for three weeks to a month each year. This distance had shaped my perception of him, often casting him as an authority figure rather than a loving parent. But on that day, something shifted. As I looked into his eyes and saw the smile forming on his face, I felt a warmth that I had long forgotten.

"Good morning," I said, my voice steady and filled with a sincerity I hadn't expressed before. In that moment, I could sense the sweetness of his demeanor and the warmth of his love and care radiating toward me. It was as if a barrier had broken down between us, allowing me to truly see him for who he was—a loving father doing his best. I realized that beneath the strict exterior was a man who cared deeply for his family, even if he sometimes struggled to express it.

As we stood there in the morning light, I felt a flicker of hope for our relationship. Maybe this was the beginning of a new chapter—one where we could reconnect, understand each other better, and build a bond that had been missing for so long.

Overwhelmed by a wave of undefinable emotions, I walked back inside our house. As I stepped up the stairs, the guilt within me intensified. In that quiet moment, I began to realize the depth of love my parents had for me and the care that my siblings, nephews, niece, and brother-in-law offered. I also thought of the unwavering support I received from my close friends—Gina, Aline, Sally, Ed, Bella, Glen, Cristy and some other friends and most importantly, my best friend Dennis. Each of them had played a significant role in my life, and I had taken their presence for granted.

As I opened the door to my room, a rush of shyness enveloped me. The emotions I had bottled up came pouring out, and I cried out loud in the stillness of the early morning. I felt the weight of my negativity over the past years, my pride in my own capabilities, and the realization that I had been searching for goodness without recognizing the trials as tests of my faith. Tears streamed down my cheeks as I bowed my head and knelt on the floor. At that sacred moment, I asked God for forgiveness—for everything I had done, for testing Him and doubting His presence in my life.

I felt a profound sense of humility wash over me, as if the burdens I had carried were slowly beginning to lift. With each tear that fell, I began to truly believe in His existence. I recognized Him as the God of all mankind and the God of the Universe. It was a revelation that filled me with hope and a renewed sense of purpose. In that vulnerable state, I committed to embracing love and gratitude, vowing to be more open to the connections I had neglected. I knew that moving forward, I wanted to cultivate deeper relationships and truly appreciate the blessings that surrounded me.

CHAPTER 6

ASSEMBLING FROM FRAGMENTS

A few weeks after my profound encounter with Jesus Christ and my realization of the struggles in my life, a new chapter began to unfold. One Sunday morning, after breakfast, I sat on a monobloc chair facing our main gate, soaking in the warmth of the day. Suddenly, I heard the familiar sound of my Aunt Liza approaching. She walked toward me, beaming with a big smile and carrying a bag of roasted pig, known as lechon.

With a joyful heart, she shared the delicious treat with us, and my mother received it with deep gratitude, her face lighting up at the gesture. After handing over the lechon, Aunt Liza sat down beside me and began a conversation that felt long overdue. "How are you? How's your eyesight going?" she asked, genuine concern evident in her voice.

It had been quite a while since we'd shared a meaningful conversation, and as she spoke, I could feel the warmth of her care. Aunt Liza began to open up, sharing her own stories—her ups and downs, her personal struggles, and the challenges she had faced throughout her life. With each word, I began to understand her better. I realized that her strictness and perfectionism were rooted in a deep desire to protect and guide those she loved. Though she may have seemed like a strict old lady, it became clear to me that she was also incredibly loving and caring.

This conversation marked a turning point in my life; I started to appreciate the small things and the people around me in a way I never had before. At that moment, surrounded by family and the warmth of connection, I felt a renewed sense of hope and gratitude. It was a reminder that every interaction holds the potential for understanding and growth, and I was eager to embrace this new perspective.

On that same day, I called our partner driver to take me to a Christian fellowship service in Mandaue City, accompanied by one of my staff members from the office. As we walked toward the venue, I was warmly welcomed by a member of the church, and I immediately felt a sense of renewal wash over me.

The atmosphere was inviting, and I found myself appreciating the messages shared by one of the pastors. I was intrigued by the teachings and eager to learn more about the Bible. After the service, I was approached by one of the life group leaders, who introduced me to the concept of the one on one session.

Despite the excitement bubbling inside me, I was also filled with doubt and fear about sharing my story with others. My confidence was lacking, and the thought of opening up made me hesitate. So, I politely ignored the offer, choosing to focus on my own journey for the time being. Still, I continued to attend the service every Sunday afternoon. Each week, I found myself more engaged, drawn in by the community and the uplifting messages. I began to see these gatherings as a vital part of my spiritual growth, offering me a sense of belonging and hope that I had been craving.

One night, while I was arranging my clothes and personal belongings in the cabinet, I stumbled upon my cardholder. Curiosity piqued, I opened it to find a PVC card adorned with letters and an image. Intrigued, I walked down to my parents' room and asked my mother about the card. She read it slowly, and I recalled her mentioning that the validity of the card had expired last August 2020. It was my Emirates residence ID card.

The revelation struck my heart like a bolt of lightning, stirring a deep longing within me. I found myself reminiscing about my time in Dubai, wishing I could return to pursue my career or perhaps even visit Canada soon.

"How I wish," I thought to myself, feeling both hopeful and nostalgic. I thanked my mother and made my way back to my room, my mind swirling with dreams of visiting the beautiful city of Dubai once again.

Just a few moments later, my phone rang. It was Dennis, calling through the Botim application. He asked how I was doing, and after a few minutes of catching up, he surprised me with an incredible offer: he invited me to visit Dubai and mentioned that I would just need someone to assist me throughout my journey. My heart swelled with joy and excitement.

"Yes! My wishes and prayers have been granted!" I thought, a mix of disbelief and happiness coursing through me. During my conversation with Dennis, I also spoke with Seraphina, who shared some news that caught my attention. She told me about her nephew, Sam who had recently undergone surgery for a condition remarkably similar to mine. Seraphina explained that the doctors discovered that the cause of his blurry vision was holes in his retina. Her sister, Vera—Sam's mother and my co-owner of Jetliner Express—had acted quickly, arranging for the surgery. I could hear the relief in Seraphina's voice as she continued, sharing that Sam's vision had significantly improved post-surgery. In fact, his eyesight was now almost 20/ 20, and he no longer needed to wear glasses. Hearing about Sam's successful recovery filled me with hope. It was a reminder that there were solutions available, and I found comfort in knowing that others had faced similar challenges and emerged victorious. Seraphina's words inspired me, and I began to consider the possibilities for my own situation. Maybe there was a path forward, and perhaps I, too, could reclaim the clarity that had eluded me for so long. The only challenge now was finding a companion for the journey. Although the idea of traveling filled me with excitement, I knew that the road ahead wouldn't be easy.

Despite my eagerness to go, the reality of my condition loomed over me, along with the restrictions imposed by every country's borders. Preparing for a flight meant navigating a maze of government and medical clearances, each step essential for ensuring my safety and compliance with regulations. I felt a mix of apprehension and determination as I considered the logistics involved. Would I have the necessary support to manage the challenges that lay ahead? I began to reach out to friends and family, hoping to find someone willing to accompany me on this important journey.

The thought of sharing this experience with someone who understood my situation brought me comfort. As I navigated through the requirements, I reminded myself that each hurdle was a step closer to my goal—reclaiming my vision and exploring the world beyond my current limitations.

Despite still experiencing sleepless nights and anxiety attacks, one November evening, I had a vivid dream about my friend Judy . She had been one of my closest managers during my time working in Cebu back in 2011. In my dream, I saw her face clearly, and we were holding hands, chatting together in a vast field covered with lush green grass. It felt like a beautiful reunion, filled with warmth and laughter.

When I woke up, the details of the dream lingered in my mind, and I couldn't shake the feeling that it was significant. Inspired by the memory of our friendship, I immediately grabbed my phone and asked Google Assistant to check if I still had Judy's contact number. To my surprise, the accessibility options on my mobile phone worked seamlessly, allowing me to find her number with ease. With a mixture of excitement and nervousness, I called Judy. As soon as she answered, I asked if she could accompany me to Dubai. At first, she thought I was joking, but I quickly reassured her of my seriousness. I struggled to convey the gravity of my current situation and the importance of having her support during this journey.

As we continued our conversation, I could sense her willingness to help. Her warmth and understanding shone through, and I felt a surge of hope. Having Judy by my side would make a world of difference, not only for the practical aspects of the trip but also for my emotional well-being. This connection felt like a sign that I was on the right path, and I was grateful for the rekindling of our friendship.

A few days after our phone conversation, she visited me in Liloan to discuss the requirements and clearances needed for our upcoming flights. We went over everything meticulously, ensuring we didn't overlook any details. Dennis, our go-to person for travel arrangements, helped us process our thirty-day short-term Dubai visa and scheduled a PCR swab test at Cebu Doctors' Hospital. With the medical test and quarantine planned for a week before our departure, I felt a wave of relief wash over me. I couldn't help but discuss all of our plans with my parents, eager to share the excitement and seek their approval. They were supportive, which gave me an added sense of confidence that everything would fall into place. I thought everything would go as smoothly as one, two, three. However, just when we thought we had everything figured out, a calamity struck our province last December 16, 2021.

That early morning, the sky was overcast, with thick, dark clouds looming overhead. I had a scheduled appointment with Judy at the quarantine center to apply for the health card needed for our upcoming trip. However, due to severe weather conditions, the quarantine center was temporarily closed, and we had to reschedule our appointment with Judy. In addition, we planned to visit my cousin in Talisay City to sign some documents on behalf of her ailing father.

We arrived at Talisay around ten o'clock in the morning, feeling a sense of urgency. My cousin Charis, the eldest daughter of my uncle Roel—my father's younger brother—was waiting for us. Meanwhile, my father was busy sorting out the land ownership of our inherited farm in Danao City. As we chatted and signed the necessary papers, I couldn't shake the feeling that the weather was shifting. The cold breeze and the heavy air seemed to signal an impending storm.

By midday, we wrapped up our meeting, but the atmosphere outside had changed drastically. We decided to head to SM Cebu City mall, approximately thirty miles from my cousin's house. With my parents, my brother Daniel, and two office staff members in tow, we made our way to the bustling mall, hoping to grab a quick lunch.

After eating, we withdrew some cash to cover the travel tax required for our journey. However, the moment we stepped inside, we felt the weight of the approaching storm.

One of my staff members saw a news alert on her Facebook feed about the disappearance of Siargao Island, a nearby province of Cebu that had been severely affected by the weather. Panic set in. We knew we had to act quickly. As I stepped out through the exit door at the north wing of SM City, the sound of the wind seemed to be whispering warnings to me.

This typhoon felt different—more menacing than others I had experienced. A sense of urgency washed over me; I needed to prepare for my family and my employees. We immediately rushed to the nearest supermarket. My mind raced with thoughts of what essentials we might need. Groceries such as can goods, noodles, bread, milk and coffee, and medicines —I was overwhelmed by the possibilities. I even withdrew additional cash, fearing the ATM machines might soon be out of service. My parents and employees were confused by my frantic actions, their expressions a mix of concern and uncertainty. I could see their bewilderment, but I was too anxious to explain.

My heart raced as I navigated the aisles, tossing items into our cart. Canned goods, instant noodles, flashlights—I grabbed everything I could think of, knowing we needed to be prepared for the worst.

As we hurried through the store, the reality of the storm began to sink in. It was no longer just an inconvenience; it was a looming threat. I could feel the tension in the air, and the urgency of our preparations heightened my anxiety.

With our cart filled to the brim, we finally checked out and loaded our supplies into the car. The wind howled outside, and I glanced at the darkening sky, a reminder of the challenge we were about to face. I knew we had to return home quickly, not just for our safety but to ensure that we were ready for whatever the storm might bring.

As we drove back, I couldn't shake the feeling that this was just the beginning. But I also felt a sense of determination. Whatever lay ahead, I was committed to protecting my family and those who depended on me. Together, we would face the storm.

As we traveled back to Liloan, the atmosphere grew increasingly tense. An airy wind whistled ominously around us, a reminder of the approaching storm. By five o'clock in the afternoon, we finally arrived at the municipality border of Liloan, and I felt a surge of urgency. I turned to Rose and Daisy, two of our office staff who had accompanied me to Cebu. "If the situation worsens, you both need to call me immediately. We'll figure out how to get you out safely," I instructed, trying to convey the seriousness of the moment. They nodded, looking both relieved and grateful as I handed them an emergency kit filled with essentials—flashlights, first aid supplies, and non-perishable snacks. I wanted them to know they were not alone. Once inside our house, I sensed that the storm was drawing closer. I asked my father to secure our family. "Let's move to the basement with the emergency kit and grocery items,"

I suggested. My mother had her own side of the house, and the only way to access her room was through a secret door that led to the basement. While she gathered supplies, I settled in the main house with our nanny, Carmen. We organized the groceries, ensuring everything was within reach. The atmosphere felt heavy with anticipation, and I couldn't shake the feeling that we were on the brink of something intense. At exactly six in the evening, the wind picked up, howling through the trees outside. The rain began to pelt against the roof, growing increasingly fierce. I glanced at Carmen, who was watching the window with a mixture of worry and determination. "Stay close," I said, trying to reassure both her and myself. "We'll be okay as long as we stay prepared." As the storm unleashed its fury, I could hear the sound of branches snapping and debris flying. I made a mental note to check on my mother and ensure she was safe in the basement. It was a strange comfort to know that we had taken the necessary precautions, but the reality of the situation weighed heavily on my mind. I knew that we had to stay calm and focused. With each passing minute, the wind and rain intensified, a constant reminder of the power of nature. But together, we were ready to face whatever the storm might bring.

Carmen and I held hands tightly, our voices united in prayer as we asked God for protection—for our family, our home, and our entire community. The intensity of Typhoon Odette was unlike anything we had ever experienced; it was the worst typhoon to hit our province in three decades.

Outside, the howling winds drowned out our voices, but I could still hear faint screams and cries for help echoing through the storm. My heart raced with fear and concern for those outside, but we knew we couldn't venture out in such dangerous conditions. Suddenly, I heard a loud crack, followed by the terrifying sound of our front roof beginning to detach from its base.

Panic surged through me as I glanced at Carmen, who was visibly shaken. "Stay calm," I urged her, trying to project a sense of strength I didn't entirely feel. Moments later, a surge of water burst through the door, flooding into my room. It poured in with such force that the staircase resembled a waterfall cascading down, creating a surreal and frightening scene.

I watched in horror as belongings began to float away, helpless against the onslaught of nature's fury. Carmen's fear deepened as she thought of her own family. "What if they're caught in this?" she whispered, her voice trembling. I could see the worry etched on her face, and it broke my heart to see her so frightened. "We need to stay strong for each other," I reassured her. "Let's focus on what we can control right now." I squeezed her hand tighter, feeling the warmth of our connection amidst the chaos.

As the storm raged on outside, we remained huddled together, praying for strength and safety. I could only hope that the cries for help would be answered, and that somehow, we would all make it through this harrowing night.

The storm finally ceased around one o'clock in the morning, leaving behind a haunting stillness. The entire area was shrouded in darkness, the only sound being the occasional drip of water as it continued to seep from the remnants of the storm.

Our home was submerged; even the bed in the basement was wet and uncomfortable, making sleep nearly impossible. At five-thirty in the morning, I woke up, heart heavy with anxiety. As I opened the door, I was met with a scene that left me in shock. The tremendous impact of Typhoon Odette was painfully evident. Our beloved mango trees had been uprooted, lying helplessly on the ground, their branches causing significant damage to our fence and parts of our house.

Photo Credit: Municipality of Liloan, https://www.facebook.com/municipalityliloancebu

Once again, my faith in the Lord was tested. In moments like these, when life seemed to unravel in unexpected ways, I found myself questioning my strength and my trust in His plan. The trials we faced felt overwhelming, as though the weight of the world was pressing down on me and my family. Yet, even in these dark moments, I knew that this test was not a punishment, but rather an opportunity to reaffirm our belief and surrender our worries to Him. It was a reminder that faith is not just about the good times, but about enduring through the storms, no matter how fierce they may be. Devastation hung in the air as I took in the full extent of the damage. A part of our roof was missing, leaving the interior vulnerable to the elements. I could hardly bear to think about what awaited me at the Jetliner Express office. With a deep breath, I made my way there. As I entered, my heart sank further. The office was flooded, water pooling around our desks, and everything was soaked—computers, printers, even crucial documents.

The chaos left in the storm's wake felt overwhelming. Stepping back outside through the main door that led to our patio, I was struck by the sheer destruction surrounding me. The ground was littered with branches, pieces of roof, and splintered wood. Our once vibrant garden had been ravaged; many of our plants had been swept away by the relentless winds, while only the strong vines of the yellow bell plants remained, defiantly clinging to the ground. As I stood amidst the wreckage, the enormity of what had just happened began to sink in.

My mother was visibly worried about the state of our property and the uncertain condition of my sister, Caryl. Determined to check on her, we decided to venture out to the main street. As we stepped through our main gate, a wave of devastation hit us. The entire area was unrecognizable—roofs were missing, electric posts lay toppled on the ground, and countless trees had been uprooted, their branches scattered like debris from a fierce battle. Despite the destruction, I turned to my mother and said, "We have to thank God. We're safe, and we still have shelter and food." Her expression softened, the weight of despair lifting slightly as hope flickered in her eyes. We walked together toward my older sister's house, taking in the wreckage around us but finding comfort in our shared purpose.

With each step, I felt a sense of resilience building between us. When we finally arrived, relief washed over us as we saw that Caryl and her family were safe, too. "Thank God!" my mother exclaimed, her voice a mixture of gratitude and relief. We embraced, grateful that despite the storm's fury, our family remained unharmed. In that moment, I realized how important it was to lean on one another during such trying times. Together, we would face the challenges ahead, finding strength in our unity and gratitude in our survival.

It was the 18th day of December, the typhoon affected transportation, making it difficult for us to get to the hospital for our swab tests. Power outages plagued the area, adding to the uncertainty. As the days went by, I checked the news anxiously, hoping the situation would improve before our scheduled flight departure on December 22. Despite the chaos, we remained determined. We reached out to local agencies for updates and tried to find alternative ways to get our clearances done.

The aftermath of the typhoon was the worst experience I could imagine. We faced a grim reality: no water, limited food supplies, total blackout, and no network connections. The ATMs were out of cash, and to make matters worse, there was no available petrol to fuel any transportation services. At that moment, I was consumed by doubt. Should I proceed with my plan to return to Dubai? "Lord, is this your plan for me? Am I meant to stay here in Cebu for good?" I pondered, standing in our backyard, surrounded by the wreckage. The uncertainty felt overwhelming, and I questioned everything. Just then, as if answering my silent plea, I suddenly got a signal on my phone after days of poor connection.

My heart raced as I saw an incoming call from Dennis. He was checking in to see if we were all okay. "Dennis!" I exclaimed, relief flooding over me. His familiar voice was a lifeline amidst the chaos. He assured me that help was being organized and that support would soon be available for those affected by the storm. As we spoke, I realized that despite the devastation surrounding us, I wasn't alone. The sense of community and connection, even in difficult times, began to fill me with hope. Perhaps staying in Cebu was part of a larger plan, one that I couldn't yet see but would eventually understand.

The miracles of God continued to shower upon us in the most unexpected ways. I was able to meet up with Judy and finalize everything for my family the day before my flight. The support from my mother, sister, and the rest of my family was invaluable. They accompanied me to Mactan Cebu International Airport, their presence a comforting reminder of home. As we arrived at the airport, I felt a mix of emotions—excitement for the journey ahead and sadness at leaving my family behind. My mother and my sister, Caryl, walked with me and Judy until we reached the security checkpoint. Their faces reflected a mixture of pride and worry, emotions that were impossible to miss. Caryl wrapped me in a tight embrace and whispered, "Be careful," her voice thick with emotion. As she pulled away, my mother stepped forward, kissing my forehead gently before enveloping me in a hug that was filled with nothing but love and concern. Tears welled up in her eyes as she held me close, and with a tremble in her voice, she said, "My son, please be careful. Take good care of yourself. I want nothing but the best for you, and I love you so much."

I could feel my own tears threatening to spill, blurring my vision as a deep wave of emotion washed over me. It was so hard to hold it together as I turned toward the entrance of the airport. Each step felt heavier, knowing that their love and concern would stay with me, even as I moved forward into the unknown. I paused for a moment, turning back to look at their faces one last time, and whispered, "Thank you, and I love you too." My voice cracked as the reality of the moment sank in, but I knew that their love would carry me through whatever lay ahead.

I took a moment to soak in the love and support surrounding me before heading into the airport. Inside, I encountered a sea of stranded passengers, each one grappling with the aftermath of the typhoon.

However, one of the immigration officers noticed me and offered assistance. With his help, I navigated through the passport border control with surprising ease. Judy was amazed at how smoothly everything went, given the chaos surrounding us. Despite the devastation in Cebu, my incomplete travel documents, and the limited short-term tourist visa, I felt a surge of gratitude. I turned to Judy and said, "Jesus made our way to Dubai." It was a statement of faith that echoed the miracles I had witnessed in the days leading up to this moment.

As I made my way to the boarding gate, I reflected on the journey that had brought me here. It hadn't been easy, but the support of my family and the divine intervention I felt throughout this ordeal filled me with hope. I was ready to embrace whatever lay ahead in Dubai, carrying the love and strength of my family with me.

The flight took about thirteen hours in total, with a layover at Clark International Airport in Pampanga. As we settled in during the stopover, I couldn't help but reminisce about the last time I had flown back to Cebu three years ago. It felt surreal to think that Jesus was now working on my prayers. I had dreamed of returning to Dubai, and now that dream was becoming a reality. With each passing hour, my excitement grew. I was looking forward to seeking medical attention to regain my vision, a crucial step in my journey. After what felt like an eternity, we finally arrived safely in Dubai. The vibrant energy of the city enveloped me, and I felt a rush of gratitude for this second chance. As I stepped out into the bustling airport, I was greeted by Dennis.

After our meet-up, we headed straight to the Holiday Inn Airport hotel, eager to spend a restful night before moving to our apartment in Oud Metha. The exhaustion from the long flight weighed heavily on me as I sank into the plush bed, grateful for a moment of peace. It was already past one o'clock in the morning, and the world outside was cloaked in darkness. The next day, we awoke around ten, sunlight streaming through the curtains. After a leisurely breakfast, we checked out and made our way to the apartment. As we stepped inside, a wave of nostalgia washed over me.

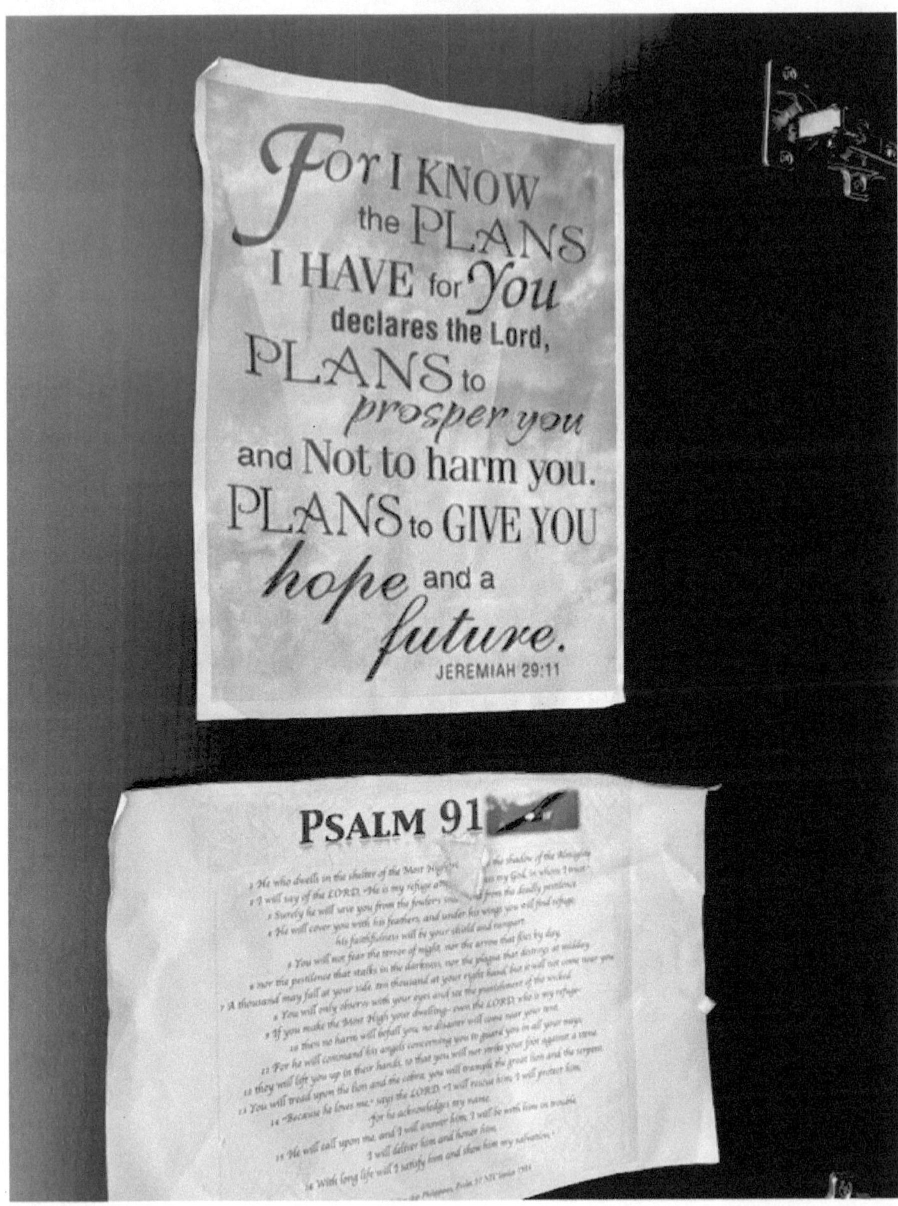

Memories flooded back—each corner of the space seemed to hold a piece of my past. As I unpacked some of my belongings, something caught my eye. A piece of paper was taped to the cabinet, its edges slightly worn but still visible. Curious, I turned to Dennis and asked him what it was. He approached with a smile, explaining that it was a very important Bible verse we had printed out when we first arrived in Dubai back in 2015. I felt a thrill of recognition as he recited the verse: "For I know the plans I have for you, declares the Lord, plans to prosper you and not to harm you, plans to give you hope and a future - Jeremiah 29:11."

Judy, standing nearby, was equally amazed that this piece of paper had remained intact after six years. As I touched the paper, a shiver ran down my spine. In the past, I had taken the message for granted, but now it resonated with a profound importance. Yet, somehow, we had persevered. This verse felt like a reminder that despite the uncertainties, there was a guiding hand at work, crafting a future filled with hope. As I reflected, I could see how our lives had unfolded.

Each challenge had shaped us, bringing us closer to who we were meant to be. The verse felt like a promise, a reassurance that we were on the right path. I glanced around the apartment, now filled with the echoes of laughter and memories we would create together. At that moment, I realized how far we had come—and how much further we could go. With renewed determination, I embraced the possibilities that lay ahead, grateful for the past but even more excited for the future.

At around four o'clock in the afternoon, Aline, along with the rest of our group, had planned a festive Christmas picnic gathering at Dubai Creek Park. The warmth of their smiles and the familiar laughter filled my heart with joy. Reunited with Aline, Dennis, Vera, Seraphina, Abdul, Kuriand Sally, with my companion Judy I felt an overwhelming sense of belonging. We shared stories, laughter, and plans for the future. I was also delighted to meet some new friends, Ruby and Yanni, who instantly added to the festive spirit of our gathering. The picnic was filled with joy and celebration, a perfect way to mark my return. Surrounded by friends, I realized that I was not just back in Dubai; I was home. With a heart full of hope and excitement, I looked forward to the new adventures that awaited me, knowing that I had a supportive community by my side.

CHAPTER 7

NEW BEGINNING

As the days passed, I found joy in the company of my friends here in Dubai, but a lingering sense of guilt and sadness weighed heavily on my heart. Leaving my family behind in Cebu felt like a constant shadow, especially knowing they had limited access to food, water, network connections, and a reliable power supply. The thought of their struggles gnawed at me, and I often found myself lost in worry. Every night, I prayed quietly, seeking comfort and strength. The flickering candlelight often illuminated my thoughts as I pleaded for my family's safety and well-being.

I cherished the moments spent with friends, but they were tinged with a bittersweet awareness of what my loved ones were enduring. Then, just before New Year's, I received the news that the power had been restored in Cebu. A wave of relief washed over me, knowing that my family would have one less burden to bear. The restoration of electricity symbolized hope and resilience, reminding me that even in the darkest times, light could find its way back.

During the first quarter of 2022, Dennis and I decided it was time to rebuild our travel agency here in Dubai. We eagerly began compiling a list of our networks in Armenia, Georgia, Turkey, the Maldives, and several other nearby countries. Our first adventure took us to the Republic of Georgia, where we planned to meet Datu, one of our business partners in Tbilisi. Upon arriving, I met Ika, Datu's tour guide and driver, who had been working in the industry for several years. Over the course of the week, we explored stunning landscapes and historic sites, immersing ourselves in the beauty of winter. Ika quickly became a good friend; we bonded over shared stories, laughter, and a sense of joy that made the trip feel even more special.

On the last day of our journey, Ika took us to a sacred monastery nestled in the mountains. He mentioned that he wanted me to meet one of the high priests of the small community. As I stepped out of the car, I was greeted by an old man wearing a black coat and a sotana. He approached me slowly, a serene smile on his face, and said, "I have been waiting for you." His words caught me off guard; we hadn't scheduled a meeting with the high priest, yet his presence felt both welcoming and significant. He took my hands gently, leading me toward the orthodox monastery, his grip warm and reassuring. As we stood in front of the stone-made altar, he began to pray.

The atmosphere was quiet and cold, yet a palpable warmth enveloped me, as if the very air around us was infused with the presence of the Holy Spirit. At that moment, I felt an overwhelming sense of peace wash over me, a profound connection that transcended words. It was as if the struggles I had been carrying melted away, replaced by a deep sense of hope and purpose.

The high priest instructed us to go to the top of the hill, where we would find water flowing beneath an ancient olive tree. He explained that this water was a symbol of purity and healing, a sacred gift that had been revered since the time of Saint Bartolome, dating back to the days of Jesus Christ. His words resonated deeply within me, heightening the sense of purpose behind our journey. Ika drove us up the winding road until we reached the crest of the hill, where the landscape unfolded into a breathtaking panorama. Dennis was awestruck by the beauty around us, the rolling hills blanketed in snow and the vast expanse of the sky above.

It felt as though we were standing on the edge of the world, surrounded by nature's majesty. Once we arrived at the olive tree, Ika helped me gather some of the precious water. As we filled our bottles, we took a moment to pray together, our voices mingling with the crisp mountain air. I closed my eyes, feeling the weight of my worries lift as we asked for complete healing and guidance. It was a moment of connection, not just with Ika and Dennis, but with something greater than ourselves.

Before we left, I carefully bottled some of the sacred water, intending to bring it back to the Philippines. It felt like a tangible piece of this extraordinary experience, a reminder of the hope and healing I had found in that sacred place. With our hearts full and spirits lifted, we began our descent, cherishing the memories we had created and the profound connections we had forged.

After a week filled with transformative experiences, we returned to Dubai brimming with happiness and positivity. The memories of our journey lingered in my heart, and Dennis took the time to help me create albums on my Facebook account. We uploaded countless photos, each snapshot a treasure I hoped to revisit one day when I regained my vision. It was a way to hold onto those moments, to keep them alive in my mind even as I faced my challenges. A few minutes later, a notification popped up on my screen. It was a comment from an old friend I hadn't heard for the past 18 years—Nerissa, one of my closest colleagues from college back in 2003. Her words instantly brought a smile to my face. She expressed how much she wanted to see me soon and mentioned that she was currently living in

California. I was touched that she had reached out after all this time. Nerissa had been in California for over a decade, working in a laboratory at the University of California General Hospital, San Diego.

As I read her message, a wave of nostalgia washed over me. I recalled our late-night study sessions, the laughter we shared, and the dreams we had for our futures. It felt like a lifetime ago. As we exchanged messages, I felt a spark of hope. I prayed to God, wishing that one day I could visit her in California. The thought of reuniting with an old friend, sharing stories of our journeys, and creating new memories together filled me with anticipation. I looked forward to the day when I could explore the beauty of California and reconnect with someone who had played a significant role in my past.

We exchanged WhatsApp numbers, and soon our nights were filled with long conversations, catching up on the years that had passed. As we reminisced about our college days, laughter filled the air, but beneath the surface, I felt a knot of anxiety tightening in my stomach. At first, I was hesitant to share my health condition. I was in a stage of denial, grappling with my fears of losing a friend. The thought of opening up about my struggles was daunting. I worried that revealing my story might lead to rejection or discrimination. Each time I considered sharing my truth, a wave of doubt washed over me. Would she still want to be my friend if she knew what I was going through? Would she see me differently? These questions haunted me, causing me to hold back for months.

Eventually, however, I knew I couldn't keep hiding. The connection we had rekindled felt too precious to risk on half-truths. Slowly, I began to unfold my story, sharing bits and pieces of my journey, my challenges, and the emotional toll it had taken on me. Each revelation brought a mixture of relief and trepidation, but I was determined to be honest with her. As I poured my heart out, I found solace in her understanding responses. Her warmth and empathy reassured me, helping to ease my fears. In that moment, I realized that true friendship could withstand even the most difficult truths. I was grateful for her patience as I navigated my vulnerabilities, and I felt a renewed sense of hope that our friendship could grow even stronger through this openness.

Our trip to Georgia was a turning point for me, symbolizing a new sense of hope. Despite everything that had happened back home in the Philippines and the challenges I faced with my disabilities, God had given me another opportunity to travel. This time, however, the experience felt different from all the others. While the joy and excitement of travel had always been special to me, this journey brought a deeper kind of fulfillment. Although I couldn't see the stunning landscapes or the beautiful faces of the people around me, God gifted me with a different kind of vision—one where my other senses were heightened and more alive.

I learned to appreciate things I had never focused on before: the feel of the air as it blew against my skin, the warmth of the sun on my face, the cold touch of the snow, and the laughter of my friends as we shared moments together. I savored the rich flavors of the local dishes and delicacies that I could taste but never see. In those moments, my sense of connection to the world deepened, not through sight, but through the emotions and sensations that filled me. I learned to appreciate the world with my heart in ways I hadn't before.

In mid-May, Dennis returned to the Philippines to visit his parents in their hometown. He stayed there for a few days before traveling to Manila to visit Gina and Aline's mother in Marikina. At that time, Aline's mother had been ill, and her health was rapidly declining. During Dennis and Gina's visit, they video-called me so that I could speak to Aline's mother. Even though I couldn't be there in person, I could still feel the warmth of her spirit through the screen. I heard her voice, and I could sense her smile as she spoke to me. Her words, though simple, touched me deeply. She told me to take care of myself,

that she wanted to see me again someday. In that brief conversation, I could feel the love and care of a mother. It was as if, despite her illness, she was offering me her blessing and wisdom. I was overwhelmed with gratitude, not only for the chance to speak to her one last time but also for the privilege of knowing such a kind and loving woman.

Aline was truly blessed to have a mother like hers—someone whose love was so genuine and selfless. I could only hope that I would have the same strength and compassion if I were ever in her shoes. That moment with Aline's mother stayed with me long after the call ended. It reminded me of the importance of family, of love, and of cherishing the people who are there for us in the hardest times. Even in the face of illness, she had given me something irreplaceable—a lesson in how to love and care for others with a deep, unwavering heart.

A few months later, life in Dubai continued to unfold with joy and new beginnings. My friends here were a constant source of support, and I cherished the great moments we shared together. Judy landed a job, which brought her a renewed sense of purpose, and I was thrilled to have secured my residency again. It felt like a fresh start for both of us. We received invitations from various friends, but one person who stood out was Seraphina. She had become like an older sister to me, always checking in to make sure I was comfortable. Seraphina would often call and visit me at the apartment, bringing with her warmth and a sense of security that made a world of difference. Her kindness reminded me that even in difficult times, I was never truly alone.

However, as the months rolled on, I began to notice a subtle disconnection with some of my other friends, particularly Aline and Sally. Once close, our interactions became less frequent, and the vibrant conversations we used to share dwindled into sporadic messages. I felt a twinge of sadness as I realized that friendships can sometimes ebb and flow, influenced by life's circumstances. Despite the joy I found with Judy and Seraphina, I couldn't shake the feeling of loss that came with drifting away from Aline and Sally. I missed the laughter and camaraderie we once enjoyed.

Dennis and I continued to strengthen our connections for our travel agency, and we began to attract more clients while exploring exciting new destinations. As his managing partner, I was entrusted with full control over operations, both in Dubai and Cebu. It was a thrilling opportunity, but it also came with its own set of challenges. One of the biggest hurdles arose when I unexpectedly lost two employees in Liloan. In a pinch, I decided to hire my sister Caryl and my brother-in-law Jeff to fill the gaps. At first, our working relationship seemed promising. We exchanged ideas and collaborated effectively, striving to improve our operations and streamline processes. There was a sense of unity as we aimed for shared goals.

However, as the months went by, the initial harmony began to unravel. Small conflicts started to emerge, often over trivial matters, and these misunderstandings snowballed into larger issues. Tensions grew, and what had once felt like a supportive environment transformed into chaos. It was heart-wrenching for my mother, who desperately wanted to see us reconcile. She often found herself in the middle, trying to mediate our disagreements and restore peace.

As the situation escalated, I struggled to control my temper. The emotional toll of navigating familial and professional dynamics took its toll on me, making it difficult to maintain a level head. I felt a mix of frustration and sadness, knowing that the relationships I cherished were becoming strained. It was a painful reminder that sometimes the people we care about most can also become the sources of our greatest conflicts.

Due to the escalating tensions, Caryl and Jeff felt compelled to resign, leaving my mother alone in our small office. This sudden change created a significant challenge, especially since my mother wasn't technically inclined and struggled with using social media to advertise job openings. In the midst of this family crisis, I turned to prayer, asking God for strength and wisdom to navigate the difficulties ahead.

Fortunately, I soon interviewed an applicant who showed remarkable eagerness for the job. Rowena, a former grade school teacher, quickly became one of my travel agents and later stepped up as my assistant. Her dedication and fresh perspective were invaluable, and with her help, we managed to bring in two more staff members to support our growing business. However, managing a business from a distance proved to be far from easy. The challenges of time differences, learning gaps, varying personalities, and even inconsistent internet connections made my role as their manager increasingly complex. It often felt overwhelming, but I was determined to push through for the sake of my family and our dreams.

A few months later, in September of that same year, I decided to visit my parents back home. To make my departure memorable, my friends organized a "despedida" party for me at the Doubletree Hotel in Al Jadaf. The hotel was buzzing with laughter and excitement as I spent one last evening with my closest friends before I left. Present that day were Dennis, Aline, Kori, Seraphina, Vera with her newborn baby Ara, her husband Abdul, Ruby, Yani, Marshie, Jason, Sam and Irene . We all stayed at the hotel overnight, filled with joy, playing games, making dance steps for TikTok, and enjoying every moment of our time together. However, the happiness of that night quickly turned into sorrow the following morning.

On the morning of September 12, I woke up to the sound of people crying in the hallway. Confused and still half-asleep, I stepped out of my room and learned that Aline's mother had passed away suddenly from a cardiac arrest. The news struck me like a lightning bolt. I was in complete shock, unsure of how to process the situation or what to do next. Aline, who had been so full of life and laughter just hours before, was now facing an unimaginable loss. My heart went out to her, and I wanted to offer my support, but at that moment, I felt helpless. I knew there was little I could do to ease her pain, but I also knew I couldn't leave her alone during such a difficult time. As a group, we rallied around Aline and did everything we could to help. We immediately began searching for a flight ticket to get her home as quickly as possible.

The urgency of the situation was palpable, but we all remained focused on supporting our friend through the chaos. After we checked out of the hotel, we drove straight to the airport. The car ride was quiet, with only the occasional murmur of comforting words being exchanged. I could see how much this loss was affecting everyone, but especially Aline. When we arrived at the airport, we gathered around her, offering our final words of encouragement and love before she boarded the flight. It was a moment of profound sadness, but also of solidarity.That day had a lasting impact on me. The fear of losing someone close, especially a beloved parent, became a very real and terrifying thought. The idea of losing my own mother or father was unfathomable. It made me realize just

how fragile life can be, and how important it is to cherish every moment with those we love. A week after it was my flight back home and I stayed for a week, yearning to reconnect with my parents, especially my mother. However, during my visit, I couldn't bring myself to speak with Caryl, Jeff, or even my niece and nephew. The conflict had escalated to a point where it created a painful rift, and I felt deeply saddened for my parents, who found themselves caught in the middle of our turmoil—a situation that should never have occurred.

After spending two days in Cebu to celebrate the Jetliner Express anniversary, I flew to Manila and then to Tagaytay, where I spent three days before heading to Baguio for a four-day vacation with my mother and Dennis. We were thrilled to reconnect with old friends, including Rex, the younger brother of Ed, who had kindly driven us when we arrived in Manila. We also spent time with Ed, Glenn and Bella, who had settled in Philippines during the midst of the pandemic, and met up with Macky and Grezlle, along with their family, who joined us in Baguio for a few days. Our time together was filled with joy, laughter, and a sense of peace, providing a much-needed escape from the family conflicts that had been weighing heavily on our hearts. As we walked through the cool mountain air of Baguio, we shared stories, reminisced about happier times, and created new memories that brought light and warmth into our lives. It was a time of renewal—a reminder of the importance of friendship, the beauty of shared moments, and the healing power of laughter amidst the challenges we were facing.

A few days later, as we returned home, I found myself sitting on our patio one evening, reflecting on the time we had spent away. It was then that my Aunt Liza stopped by for a visit. We shared a pleasant conversation, catching up on life, and I made sure to greet her with a belated happy birthday. I could still clearly remember her few last words before she left me on the patio. She smiled warmly and said, "I am very happy with who you are right now, especially after all the struggles you've faced these past few years. Thank you for not forgetting my birthday, and always take care of yourself. Tita loves you so much." Her words stayed with me long after she left, filling me with gratitude and warmth. It was a reminder of how much she cared for me and how far I had come, despite the challenges I had faced. The love and support from those closest to me were more meaningful than ever, and I felt deeply grateful for the bond we shared. It was a small yet meaningful moment, reminding me of the importance of family bonds and the love that continued to exist amidst the challenges we faced.

After a quick vacation, we returned to Dubai, ready to focus on various errands and reconnect with friends. We attended several gatherings, but one event that stood out vividly was Kori's birthday celebration at the Pearl Resort in Omal Queen. Ruby, Seraphina, and Yanni had invited us to join, which I was looking forward to—until I found out a little secret on the shuttle ride there. As we settled into our seats, Seraphina leaned in and whispered to me, "Clark, please extend your patience with Kuri. You're actually not invited, but I insisted you to come since you're part of our circle." Her words hit me like a cold wave. I felt a wave of disappointment wash over me, a sudden realization that I didn't truly belong to this group as I had once thought. As the party began, I struggled with feelings of disconnection from what I had considered my close friends. However, I took a deep breath, stayed calm, and tried my best to enjoy the moments, reminding myself that I was still grateful to be included.

The next day, while packing my things in my room after breakfast, I was surprised to find Aline, Sally, Seraphina, Ruby, and Dennis all gathered inside to check me out. Their lively chatter filled the room as they excitedly discussed plans for an upcoming international trip to Armenia, where they intended to spend Christmas together. It stung a little when I realized that Dennis and I hadn't been invited initially, but then Seraphina and Kuri turned to us with sincere smiles, extending an invitation for us to join them. At that moment, I felt a warmth in their sincerity that melted away the earlier discomfort. It was a reminder that friendships can sometimes be messy but also filled with genuine intentions. We quickly made the decision to book our flight tickets to Yerevan, excited for the adventure that awaited us. This unexpected opportunity felt like a fresh start, a chance to rekindle connections and create new memories with friends who truly wanted us there.

However, the excitement of the trip quickly turned into insecurities. Dennis, due to work commitments, couldn't join us on the first day. He suggested that I fly with them on the first day instead. At first, I was excited about the idea, looking forward to being with everyone right from the start. But then, Seraphina informed me that Aline, and Kuri didn't want me to join them initially. They were concerned that my disabilities might prevent me from keeping up with the group, that I might not be able to stand or manage the physical demands of the trip. I was hurt by their words, but what hurt even more were the messages I received on our WhatsApp group.

The conversations were painful to read—full of discussions and decisions that seemed to exclude me. It wasn't just about the trip; it felt like they weren't considering me as a friend, but rather as a burden. The lack of care and understanding stung deeply. I felt like an outsider, and the bond I thought we shared began to feel fragile and distant. After reflecting on it, I made the difficult decision not to join them on the first day. Instead, I chose to join them on the second day of the trip, when Dennis would be there, and I could feel more at ease. But even as I made that choice, I couldn't shake the feeling that something had shifted—something irreparable. I realized that this moment, this exclusion, was the beginning of the slow unraveling of my connection with those I had considered my closest friends. The discrimination I felt because of my disabilities hit me hard. It wounded my pride in a way I hadn't expected.

I had always prided myself on being strong, independent, and capable, and to be told that my limitations could hold others back left me feeling both small and rejected. It wasn't just about not being able to join them on the first day—it was about being seen differently, as someone who could no longer fully participate, no longer fit into the plans or the group dynamic. At that moment, I began to question my place among them. I wondered if they truly valued me for who I was, or if I had simply become an afterthought, someone to be tolerated but not fully embraced. The feeling of being excluded, not because of my personality or my worth as a person, but because of my disability, was a painful realization that would stay with me long after the trip.

After that difficult experience during our Armenia trip, Dennis invited me to visit Israel and spend Christmas there with our other friends and clients. It was his way of helping me escape the feelings of desperation I had been carrying. The idea of visiting Israel was not only exciting but also deeply meaningful. It became another unforgettable chapter in my life. On December 25th, we visited Bethlehem—the birthplace of Jesus Christ. The church was packed with people from all over the world, each of us united in our reverence for this holy place. Bethlehem, located in the Palestinian territories, is an area where Muslims have long been the majority, yet despite the longstanding history of conflict between Israel and Palestine, there was a palpable sense of peace in that sacred space. As I stood in the church, I could feel the weight of history all around me, but also a profound sense of unity and shared faith.

The most remarkable moment came when I had the chance to touch the Star of Bethlehem, the very spot where it is believed Jesus was born. As my fingers made contact with the star, an overwhelming wave of emotion rushed over me. Tears began to flow down my cheeks, and I felt a deep connection to the love of our Lord Jesus Christ. The experience was indescribable—words could not capture the sense of peace, love, and grace that filled my heart in that sacred moment. We stayed in Jerusalem for a week, and during that time, we visited several other significant locations. We traveled to Nazareth, where Jesus spent his childhood, and to the Sea of Galilee, where many of his miracles took place. We also visited the Jordan River, where I was baptized by one of the priests. Being baptized in such a historic and holy place was a deeply emotional experience that strengthened my faith and renewed my sense of purpose.

Lastly, we explored the Old City of Jerusalem, where history and spirituality converge at every corner. Each of these places felt like stepping into the pages of the Bible, not just as a witness, but as someone experiencing the very sacrifices and teachings of Jesus. Walking through these sacred sites made the Bible come to life in ways I had never imagined. I felt as though I was part of the story, feeling the weight of Christ's sacrifices and the love that underpins it all. It was an experience that deepened my faith and left an indelible mark on my heart. In those moments, I felt a profound sense of peace and connection to something greater than myself, a reminder that despite the struggles we face, there is always hope, love, and redemption.

After our incredible journey through Israel, we returned to Armenia, where we were fortunate to meet new friends, including Naira, who would soon become a business partner. Naira took us on a tour of some of Armenia's most breathtaking landscapes and historic sites. We visited the Temple of Garni, an ancient pagan temple set against a dramatic backdrop of mountains. We explored Noravank, a stunning monastery complex with red rock cliffs, and the Armenia Alphabet Monument, a tribute to the country's unique alphabet. We also visited Mount Ararat, the symbolic peak that towers over the region, and the St. John the Baptist Church, a peaceful place of reflection and worship. One of the most moving places we visited was the Genocide Memorial, which commemorates the victims of the Armenian Genocide, a tragedy that deeply shaped the nation's history. We saw so much during that second visit—each place filled with its own stories and significance.

This second trip to Armenia marked a turning point for me. It ignited a new sense of determination and a desire to take my business to the international market. I could feel that my horizons were expanding, and the trip gave me fresh perspectives on growth and opportunity. I shared my travel experiences with my employees, telling them about the places I'd seen and the people I had met. I also stayed in touch with my mother, keeping her updated on my travels through phone calls and video chats. Sharing these moments with my loved ones helped bridge the distance between us, even as I was far from home. But just as I was beginning to feel a sense of peace and excitement about the future, tragedy struck again. I received the devastating news that my aunt Liza had passed away due to complications from breast cancer. Her internal organs had been affected, and despite the efforts of doctors, she couldn't survive. I was in shock. My heart broke, and I wanted nothing more than to be with my family to mourn and pay my respects, but financial constraints kept me from returning home. The reality of being so far away, unable to offer support or be there in person, filled me with deep regret. In my sorrow, I turned to prayer. Though I couldn't be there physically, I offered nine nights of prayer each evening for my aunt's soul and for strength for my family. It became a way for me to cope with my helplessness, even though the pain of being so far away was overwhelming.

The news of my aunt's passing stirred up a new wave of fear and anxiety. The thought of losing another loved one—especially someone as dear as my aunt—brought back all the negative thoughts I had tried so hard to push aside. Once again, the fear of loss and the feeling of helplessness took root. I found myself unable to sleep properly, lying awake at night, feeling the anxiety attack creeping up on me. It was as if the weight of the world had shifted, and I couldn't escape it. The anxiety began to feel all-encompassing, and I realized that, despite the distance, grief and fear could still find a way to reach me.

During my mourning, I found little support from my so-called friends, except for Dennis and Seraphina. This deepened my feelings of isolation and added to the growing resentment I was feeling toward them. Seraphina tried to explain it to me—she said that Aline and the others simply weren't interested in my stories or what I was going through. Her words cut deeper than I expected. I couldn't understand why the people I had considered close friends would be so distant when I needed them the most. I asked myself over and over, *What have I done to deserve this?* I began to hate myself. I hated the fact that I was blind, that I couldn't see the world as others could. If only I had normal senses, if only I had a decent job or a different life, maybe things would be different. Maybe then I wouldn't be so vulnerable to discrimination and rejection. The anger and self-loathing began to consume me. I felt as though my entire body was covered in insecurities, my heart weighed down with hatred for myself and for the way I felt abandoned by those I had trusted.

But one night, as I lay in bed, something remarkable happened. I had just fallen asleep when I suddenly woke up to an intense, glowing light beside my bed. A man stood there, radiating brightness, but I couldn't make out his face. He wasn't someone I recognized, and yet, his presence felt both powerful and peaceful at the same time. Without saying a word, he reached out and gently touched my forehead. As soon as he did, I felt a wave of calm wash over me, and I drifted back into sleep, as if nothing had happened. At first, I thought I had been dreaming. But the more I thought about it, the more I knew that it was real. At that moment, I knew, without a doubt, that Jesus had come to me again.

For the second time, I had felt His presence—felt His touch—reminding me that I wasn't truly alone. That somehow, in my deepest pain and despair, He was there, guiding me, comforting me, showing me that I was loved. The encounter left me shaken, but also filled with a sense of peace that I couldn't explain. It was as if all the fears, doubts, and insecurities I had been carrying were momentarily lifted, and I felt a renewed sense of hope. I knew that Jesus had reached out to me in my darkest moment, not because I was perfect or deserving, but because I was His—and that was enough.

The next day, as I sat in my room feeling lost in my thoughts, I turned on the television to distract myself. I stumbled upon a TV series, and surprisingly, the topic of that particular episode was about forgiveness. As I watched, the words and the message struck me deeply, like a sudden awakening. The show focused on the struggle of letting go of pain and forgiving those who had hurt us. It felt as though God Himself had placed that message in front of me at the exact moment I needed to hear it. The episode made me think of all the people who had caused me so much pain—people I had trusted and considered close friends. It reminded me of the unresolved hurt I carried inside, especially the distance that had grown between me and Aline. I realized that the bitterness I felt was keeping me trapped in my own sorrow, and I knew I had to let go. Forgiving them wasn't easy, but I understood that it was something I needed to do, not for them, but for my own peace of mind and soul. It was incredibly difficult to even think about forgiveness.

The pain was still fresh, and the wound had not fully healed. But as the days passed, the weight of the hurt began to lessen little by little. It wasn't a quick fix, but I could feel the bitterness starting to deplete, as if I was slowly freeing myself from its hold. One day, I asked Seraphina if she could help me talk to Aline. I wanted to have an honest conversation with her, to tell her how I felt and perhaps clear the air between us. But Seraphina confronted me with a reality I wasn't ready for: Aline didn't want to talk, and she didn't like confrontation. She preferred to avoid difficult conversations rather than face them head-on. That was a hard pill to swallow. I had hoped for some kind of resolution, some opportunity for healing, but it became clear that Aline wasn't ready to engage.

So, I let it go—for the time being. I had no choice but to leave it behind, even though the pain of being distant from her remained. I realized that, sometimes, the healing process is more about accepting the situation as it is than forcing things to be what we want them to be. There were a few invitations to gatherings at Aline's house after that, but the atmosphere was always cold and distant. I didn't feel like part of the group anymore. I would sit quietly in the corner, observing everything around me, feeling the gap between us grow wider with each passing moment. People were talking, laughing, but I felt disconnected, as if I wasn't truly seen anymore.

The only person who reached out to me during these gatherings was Sally. She was the one who made an effort to speak with me, to entertain me, to make me feel less invisible. I appreciated her kindness, but even her company couldn't fill the emptiness I felt in that space. It was a difficult period of my life, and every day seemed like a reminder of what had been lost. Yet, through it all, I held on to the hope that somehow, in time, things would heal—either with Aline or in my heart. Until then, I knew I had to focus on forgiving, even when it was the hardest thing to do.

During this time, I also began reaching out to my Aunt Leoni, who lives in England, through Messenger. Although part of me wanted to reconnect, there was still a nagging voice in my head, reminding me of the painful things she had said to me during my time in the Philippines. I remembered the harsh words she had spoken—how I was a burden to my family and to those around me. Those words still stung, echoing in the back of my mind whenever I thought of her. But despite the hurt, I made a conscious decision to try to fight the negativity that lingered in me. I knew I had to replace those painful memories with forgiveness, even if it was hard. So, I pushed through the emotional weight and continued the conversation with her, hoping to rebuild some of the lost connection. We exchanged messages, trying to catch up on the time we had missed, but there were moments when the old feelings resurface.

My aunt would often question my mission in Dubai, and the purpose of my business. Her doubts seemed to undermine the journey I was on, making me feel like my efforts were insignificant or misunderstood. Once again, I felt the sting of discrimination—this time from someone in my own family. The sadness crept back into my heart. The sense of being undervalued and questioned for the choices I had made added to the emotional burden I was already carrying. It seemed like the discrimination I had faced—whether from friends, family, or society—kept following me, no matter where I went or what I tried to achieve. I started to wonder if I would ever be truly accepted for who I was, or if I would always be seen through the lens of my disabilities.

During this period, my perspective on sharing my experiences online also began to shift. At first, I had used Facebook to document my travels and share positive moments, a way to create memories and connect with others. But soon, my posts weren't just about sharing joy—they became a way for me to prove something to the people who had doubted me. I wasn't just sharing my experiences; I was trying to show the world, especially those who had looked down on me, that I was capable of more than they thought. I wanted to prove that despite my disabilities, I could still travel the world, pursue my dreams, and live a full life. I became so consumed by this need to prove myself that I started posting not to create memories or share good vibes, but to boast—to show everyone who had ever doubted me that I was more than their assumptions.

The pride I felt in my accomplishments began to spill over into my social media presence. I was no longer just celebrating the joy of travel; I was fighting back against the limitations others had placed on me. In doing so, I realized that my posts had become a kind of defense mechanism, a way to say, *Look at me. See what I'm capable of, even if you don't understand it.* But as I continued down this path, I couldn't shake the feeling that my motivation had shifted from authentic joy to an attempt to prove something to others—and perhaps to myself. The line between pride and boastfulness had blurred, and I wondered if this newfound sense of "validation" was truly what I needed or just a reflection of my ongoing struggle with self-worth.

On the evening of February 9, Seraphina called us, inviting Dennis and me to meet her at Sahara Mall in Sharjah. We were excited to catch up, so we made our way there, looking forward to a nice dinner and perhaps a movie afterward. It had been a while since we last spent time together, and we all needed a break from the routine. The evening was warm, filled with laughter and good conversation. We had a great time bonding over our meal, chatting about life, work, and the things that matter most. After dinner, we decided to watch a movie, which made the night even more enjoyable. The film was a lighthearted escape from the usual grind, and it helped to lift our spirits. As the movie came to an end, we realized that the night had flown by. It was already well past midnight when we decided it was time to head to Seraphina's place. She lived in Al Taawun, Sharjah, with Ed's family, so we hailed a taxi and made our way there. The ride was quiet at first, but as we approached Seraphina's home, she suddenly turned to us, her voice tinged with frustration and sadness. "I need to talk to you both," she said, her tone more serious than usual. Dennis and I exchanged a glance, sensing that something was weighing heavily on her. As we arrived at the restaurant near her residential building, Seraphina led us inside and sat us down. It didn't take long before she began to open up, her emotions spilling out in a way we hadn't expected. She had been planning a trip with her friend Aline to the Netherlands, something they had both been looking forward to for months. They had even started making arrangements to apply for their visas together, excited for the adventure ahead. But then, something happened that left Seraphina heartbroken. She had found out that Aline had already left for the Netherlands—but not with her. Aline had gone on the trip with another friend named Raine, leaving Seraphina behind without any explanation.

The betrayal was too much for her to bear, and it had left her feeling abandoned and alone. Seraphina had trusted Aline, and to find out she'd been left out in such a way was a deep blow to her. Listening to her, I could feel the weight of her disappointment. It wasn't just about the trip; it was about the broken trust and the hurt that comes with realizing someone you cared about had let you down. Seraphina's eyes were filled with tears as she spoke, and I couldn't help but feel a deep sense of sadness for her. Dennis and I were both silent for a moment, letting her express her feelings without interruption. Sometimes, all you need is someone to listen, and that's exactly what we tried to provide. We sat with her, giving her our full attention as she poured her heart out. It was clear that she needed to share her frustrations, and we wanted to be there for her at that moment.

As Seraphina continued, we offered words of comfort, reminding her that she wasn't alone. We reassured her that her feelings were valid, and that even though Aline's actions were hurtful, it didn't define her or her worth. Sometimes, people make choices that hurt others, but that doesn't mean Seraphina deserved that treatment. We let her speak as much as she needed to, knowing that sometimes the best way to heal from emotional pain is to let it out. After a long while, Seraphina seemed a little calmer, though the sadness still lingered in her eyes. I could see that the hurt wouldn't disappear overnight, but at least she had shared it with us, and that was the first step toward moving forward.

By the time we left, it was nearing 3 a.m., but I knew Seraphina would be okay. She had gone through a lot of emotional ups and downs, but at least she had people around her who cared. People who would always be there when she needed them most. Just before we parted ways, Seraphina made one more request that caught me off guard. She asked Dennis if he could lend her money so she could fly to the Netherlands and finally take the trip she had dreamed of. The request hung in the air for a moment, and I could sense a shift in the tone of the conversation. Dennis, though sympathetic, didn't commit to anything that night. He knew Seraphina had outstanding debts from previous years, and lending her money didn't feel like the right choice—especially given her current situation. He gently declined, explaining that he wasn't in a position to help financially. I could tell it was a difficult decision for him, but we both reassured her that we would support her in any other way we could—just not with money.

As we made our way home that night, the quiet of the drive gave me plenty of time to reflect. I couldn't stop thinking about the emotional weight of the evening, the frustration Seraphina had been carrying, and the way her request seemed to come out of nowhere. It left me wondering about her true motives. Was her plea for money a result of her hurt and disappointment?

Or was there something deeper driving her to ask for such a significant favor at such a vulnerable moment? I didn't have all the answers, but the questions lingered, as I realized how complex our relationships can be—filled with moments of support, but also moments of uncertainty and unspoken tension.

The next morning, we received an invitation from Seraphina to visit her at her place. She seemed to want more support, and we were happy to spend time with her and offer some comfort. When we arrived at her apartment, we were welcomed by Seraphina at the door with a faint smile. Inside, Vera was there as well, along with her baby, Ara, whose innocent laughter filled the room, providing a brief moment of lightness amidst the heavy atmosphere. Seraphina invited us to sit on the couch, and we settled in, exchanging pleasantries. But it wasn't long before the conversation turned serious again. Seraphina still seemed burdened by the emotional weight of her recent experience with Aline, and we could tell that her heart wasn't light.

A few minutes later, Ruby arrived. It was clear that she had come to offer comfort too, and she quickly joined us in supporting Seraphina. We all listened patiently as Seraphina spoke about her ongoing frustrations and the disappointment she still felt. Her pain was palpable, and as much as we tried to reassure her, we knew that her healing would take time. She appreciated our presence, but there was still a part of her that seemed stuck in the hurt of being betrayed by someone she had trusted so deeply. Then, Seraphina made the same request again. She asked Dennis if he could lend her money, so she could fly to the Netherlands and finally take the trip she had dreamed of. It was the second time she had asked, and her voice this time carried more urgency, as though she felt desperate for something to change. Dennis, however, gently refused.

He understood the difficult emotions she was facing, but he also knew that lending money wasn't the right solution, especially given Seraphina's existing financial situation and past debts. He wanted to help in a way that would truly benefit her in the long run, not just provide a temporary escape. Seeing how much Seraphina still needed a change, Dennis and I decided to offer something different. "What if we planned a getaway together?" I suggested.

"A weekend trip to the Maldives, all expenses paid. Just the three of us, if she wants to come—so we can relax, recharge, and take a break from all the stress." Seraphina's eyes brightened at the idea, and for the first time that day, she seemed to lift from the heaviness she'd been carrying. We quickly booked flights and a hotel, organizing everything for a weekend escape to the Maldives. The idea of a few days of sun, sand, and sea seemed like just what Seraphina needed to help her regain some perspective and healing.

And so, just two weeks later, we were all on a plane together, heading for an unforgettable trip. In the Maldives, the beauty of the islands worked its magic. We spent our days lounging on the beach, enjoying the warmth of the sun, swimming in the crystal-clear water, and exploring the serene surroundings. Seraphina seemed to shed the emotional burden she had been carrying for weeks, her laughter returning, and the weight in her heart lifting, even if just for a little while. It wasn't just about the trip—it was about offering Seraphina a break from the pain, a chance to rediscover joy, and an opportunity to recharge. We all bonded deeply during that time, and by the end of the weekend, Seraphina seemed more at peace. The trip had given her the space she needed to heal and reminded her that no matter how difficult life could be, there would always be moments of joy, connection, and renewal.

After the incredible time we spent in the Maldives, we weren't ready to stop exploring and enjoying new experiences together. So, we planned another trip—this time to Hong Kong and Macao, eager to immerse ourselves in even more adventure and culture. Before our flight to Hong Kong, Ruby and Yani accompanied us to the airport. But also knowing that we had new experiences, memories, and stories to look back on. As we waited for our flight, we found a quiet spot in the airport cafeteria to sit down and relax. The noise of the airport buzzed around us, but at that moment, it felt as though time had slowed. We began talking about the future, and it was during this time that the topic of relocating to Canada came up.

But now, with everything we had been through—supporting each other, facing challenges, and growing stronger as a group—the idea of a fresh start somewhere new felt more real than ever. "We need to start planning seriously," Ruby said. "Once you guys get back from this trip, we should begin looking at the options for moving to Canada." We all agreed that it was time to take the next step. We talked about the potential pathways for immigration, including the various visa options and programs. Ruby had some knowledge about the process, and Seraphina, who had been researching the topic in her spare time, was already familiar with a lot of the details.

We spent the next hour or so discussing everything from job opportunities to financial planning. "We'll need to save up more, figure out where we'd like to settle, and really understand the costs involved," Dennis said, his eyes bright with anticipation. "But it's not just about the money. It's about building a new life—creating a future where we can all grow and thrive." The conversation shifted between practicalities and dreams. We talked about the kind of work we'd be looking for once we were settled in Canada. The more we talked, the clearer the picture became: relocating to Canada wasn't just an idea anymore; it was a goal we were going to make happen. We also discussed the financial side of things, which would undoubtedly be one of the biggest challenges.

We flew from Dubai to Hong Kong aboard Cathay Pacific, which made for a smooth and comfortable journey. Upon arrival, we were excited to meet Sharon, Seraphina's cousin, who was kind enough to show us around and share her insider knowledge of the area. Our days in Hong Kong were filled with excitement and awe as we explored some of the city's most iconic and beautiful spots. We started with a visit to the Avenue of Stars, a picturesque promenade with stunning views of Victoria Harbour and the Hong Kong skyline, where we snapped photos and admired the famous handprints of Hong Kong's movie legends. From there, we made our way to Ngong Ping 360, where we took a breathtaking cable car ride high above the lush landscapes to reach the Ngong Ping Village and the majestic Tian Tan Buddha.

Next, we headed to Victoria Peak, the highest point on Hong Kong Island, where the panoramic views were simply unforgettable. We even rode the famous Peak Tram, an iconic funicular that ascends the steep incline, offering us incredible views of the city below. The sight of Hong Kong's towering skyline and bustling harbor was mesmerizing from up there. Our adventures continued at Disneyland Hong Kong, where we let our inner children roam free.

From thrilling rides to the charming parades and fireworks, the park was a magical escape that brought laughter and joy to all of us. Ocean Park, with its combination of marine life exhibits and adrenaline-pumping rides, was another highlight of our trip. We spent hours there, exploring the various zones, from the Marine World to the roller coasters, and even took a moment to relax and watch the pandas. When it came to food, we were in for a treat. We dined at some of the best traditional Hong Kong restaurants, savoring iconic dishes like dim sum, wonton noodles, and roast goose. Every meal was a feast, and it felt like a celebration of the city's rich culinary heritage. As night fell, we wandered the streets of Mongkok Night Market, where the neon lights lit up the bustling market filled with street food, trinkets, and local fashion. The energy of the market was contagious, and we spent hours strolling through the maze of stalls, sampling snacks and enjoying the vibrant atmosphere.

After a few unforgettable days in Hong Kong, we decided to cross the border and take a quick tour of Macau, a city known for its rich history, glamorous hotels, and sprawling casinos. We wandered through the Ruins of St. Paul's, a UNESCO World Heritage site, and marveled at the blend of Portuguese and Chinese influences that defined the city. We also visited some of the iconic Macau casinos, such as The Venetian Macao and Wynn Palace, Parissian where we admired the extravagant architecture and enjoyed the lively atmosphere. It was an exciting but short visit, a perfect way to wrap up our journey before heading back.

Overall, our time in Hong Kong and Macau was nothing short of spectacular. We created memories that would last a lifetime—together, experiencing the best of both cities, indulging in their beauty, culture, and excitement. It felt like the perfect continuation of our friendship and the healing journey we had started in the Maldives.

After having breakfast at our hotel, we checked out and headed to Hong Kong International Airport to catch our flight to Dubai. But when we arrived at the check-in counter, we were met with some unexpected and troubling news from the check-in officer. It felt like another test of faith and friendship. The officer informed us that the airline could not allow us to board the flight due to their no-show policy. The original ticket we purchased was for a connecting flight from Dubai to Cebu, with a layover in Hong Kong, and the reverse journey. However, we had decided not to continue to Cebu and to stay only in Hong Kong. Dennis immediately tried to negotiate with the Cathay Pacific officer, explaining our situation, but we were told that it was impossible to change the booking and take just the last segment of the flight. To make matters worse, we were informed that in order to take the flight to Dubai, we would need to pay 8,000 Dirhams for all three of us. The situation felt overwhelming, and it was a moment of uncertainty and frustration. We stood there, unsure of what to do next, but it was a reminder of how unexpected challenges could arise even when things seemed to be going smoothly. I immediately asked Seraphina to checked other airlines maybe we can find cheaper flights to Dubai. However she put her luggage away from me.

At that moment, I realized that Seraphina was more concerned with her own need to return quickly than with the situation Dennis and I were in. I couldn't help but feel that she had no real concern for the financial strain this was putting on Dennis, especially after everything we had done to support her during the trip. But I kept my feelings to myself. I didn't want to escalate the situation or make it worse. Dennis, being the calm and level-headed person he is, didn't say much either. He simply agreed to the rebooking and paid the amount needed to secure our seats. It was frustrating, but at that point, there wasn't much we could do. We all wanted to return to Dubai, and sometimes you just have to accept that some things are out of your control.

By the end of the day, after what felt like endless waiting and back-and-forth with the airline staff, we finally boarded the flight back to Dubai on Cathay Pacific. The cabin crew greeted us with their usual warmth, but I could sense that the mood among us had shifted slightly. The carefree joy we'd experienced in Hong Kong seemed distant now, replaced by the pressure of the unexpected cost and the emotional strain of the situation.

As we settled into our seats on the plane, I couldn't shake the feeling that something had changed during the last few hours of our trip. Seraphina was no longer the person I had shared so many happy moments with; she seemed distant and focused only on her own immediate needs. It was hard not to feel a little resentful, but I kept my thoughts to myself, choosing to focus on getting home. Despite the tension of the final day, the memories of the trip were still fresh in my mind—the beauty of Hong Kong, the joy we had shared in the Maldives, and the laughter we'd experienced together.

I reminded myself that no friendship was perfect, and sometimes, issues arise that test our patience and understanding.

When we finally landed in Dubai, the weight of the situation seemed to lift slightly, but the tension remained. The trip had been unforgettable in so many ways, but the way it ended left me with mixed emotions. I couldn't help but wonder how our friendship would be affected by the events that had unfolded in those final hours. When we finally arrived back in Dubai, things were far from smooth. As part of our plan to resolve the inconvenience with the flight, Dennis and Seraphina had agreed that Seraphina would take charge of handling the refund request and addressing the complaints with Cathay Pacific.

After all, it was her booking that had caused the issue in the first place, and she had assured us that she would take care of it once we were back. But as the days passed, it became clear that Seraphina had not followed through on her end of the agreement. Despite several reminders, she didn't take any action. Dennis, who was already swamped with his busy schedule, became increasingly frustrated. The refund was a matter of principle, and more importantly, it was money that we all needed to get back.

After waiting for nearly a week, he finally decided to take matters into his own hands. He submitted the refund request himself, which took up a considerable amount of his time and energy. During that week, Ruby and I sat down to talk about our Canada plans—a dream we had been discussing for weeks. We were excited about the prospect of starting a new life there, and it was a relief to focus on something positive after everything that had happened. But as we chatted about the practicalities of our move, Ruby casually mentioned something that stopped me in my tracks. Ruby said, "Seraphina and Dennis had an agreement about her show money—the part of her travel documentation needed for visa purposes." My heart skipped a beat. I didn't understand. Show money? I turned to Ruby, who explained further.

Apparently, Seraphina had been bragging to her and Yani about how Dennis had agreed to help her with the money she needed to prove she could financially support herself for her travels. Ruby said it had come up in conversation, and Seraphina had acted as if the deal was already done. Dennis was completely unaware of this agreement, and when he found out, he was deeply shocked. The more he thought about it, the more he realized that Seraphina had never mentioned this arrangement to him directly. Not only had she failed to mention it, but she had also gone ahead and discussed it with Ruby and Yani, without consulting him first. It felt like a breach of trust, especially considering that Seraphina had made a number of financial requests throughout the trip, including the loan she had asked Dennis. Dennis immediately confronted Seraphina, sending her a direct message, questioning why she had shared such private financial matters with Ruby and Yani without informing him first. The message was calm, but there was a sense of frustration beneath his words.

That moment of confrontation marked the beginning of a breakdown in the friendship. Seraphina didn't take the message well. She felt betrayed, hurt, and accused us of airing out her personal business. In turn, she became distant, even hostile, and the tension between her and the rest of us grew. It didn't take long for things to escalate—Seraphina became openly resentful, especially towards Ruby and me, accusing us of meddling in matters that didn't concern us. What followed was the gradual unraveling of the bond we had all shared during the trip. Seraphina's anger seemed to fester, and soon, it wasn't just about the flight issue or the show money—it was about everything that had happened during our time together.

Every conversation seemed to turn into an argument, and even the simplest misunderstandings grew into massive conflicts. We were stuck in a cycle of resentment, and it began to feel like our plans for the future were slipping away. Ruby, Dennis and I were all heartbroken by the growing divide between our circle. What had started as a dream to build a new life in Canada now felt like an impossible goal. The friendship that had once been so strong was now fraying at the edges, and we were forced to face the painful reality that things might never go back to the way they were.

After days of tension, Dennis and I came to a painful decision: we would put our Canada plans on hold. It wasn't that we didn't still want to go—deep down, we did—but the emotional weight of the situation had become too much to bear. Our friendship with Seraphina seemed irreparably damaged, and it was hard to imagine starting a new life in a foreign country when we couldn't even resolve the issues we were facing here in Dubai. The weight of the conflict was just too heavy, and the dream of Canada, at least for now, felt out of reach. That was the turning point. The trip to Hong Kong and everything that had followed had opened our eyes to some harsh truths about our relationships. The conflicts, the misunderstandings, and the emotional toll had taken a toll on all of us. Seraphina's behavior had left us questioning the foundation of our friendship, and in the end, we had to decide what was more important—our dreams of a new life or the fractures in the relationships that had once felt so strong.

A week after the tensions between our circle reached their peak, things didn't seem to be getting any easier. Dennis was still processing the fallout from the situation with Seraphina, and now, he faced another hurdle—his US visa interview. It had been something he'd been looking forward to for a while, as he was planning to travel for work opportunities, and the US had always been a destination on his list. With a sense of quiet determination, Dennis made his way to the US Embassy in Dubai for the interview. He had prepared well, and he was hopeful, despite the emotional strain from the recent events. He knew how important this step was for his future, but nothing could have prepared him for the outcome. The interview didn't go as expected. Dennis was informed that his application had been rejected. The reason cited was his limited travel history—the fact that he had not traveled widely, particularly to countries like those in Europe, which were often seen as a stepping stone to the US. The officer explained that the US Embassy needed to see a broader track record of international travel to ensure that applicants would return to their home country after their visit. The rejection stung deeply. After all the effort, time, and energy spent preparing for the interview, it felt like a crushing blow. But Dennis surprised me with his response. He didn't let his frustration show. Instead, he remained calm, collected, and determined to move forward. He knew that this wasn't the end of the road—just a setback. "Don't worry," he said quietly, after hearing the news. "It's just a step. We'll figure it out." Despite his calm demeanor, I could tell that Dennis was disappointed. He had put so much into the idea of traveling to the US, and now, the future seemed uncertain again. The weight of the rejection was hard to ignore, but his attitude remained positive—he was not going to let this one experience dictate his future. Determined to move past the setback, we began researching alternative paths to secure a

US visa. We contacted different visa consultants and sought advice from those who had successfully navigated the application process. Ruby and I also offered as much support as we could, knowing how important this dream was to him.

After speaking to a number of consultants, we were finally given a new direction. One of the US visa consultants suggested a fresh approach: instead of trying to go straight to the US, Dennis should first travel to Europe—specifically, to Turkey—and establish a more substantial international travel history. From there, we could apply for a Spain Schengen visa, which would grant Dennis access to several European countries. This would help him build the kind of travel profile the US Embassy was looking for, and it would make his future applications more likely to succeed. It was a solid plan, and one that brought a new sense of hope. It wasn't the direct route Dennis had hoped for, but it was a path forward—one that required patience and strategy. We were relieved to have a new plan to work with, and Dennis was determined to follow it through. So, we started preparing for the next leg of the journey. We booked our flights to Turkey, ready to explore a new country and gain the international travel experience needed to strengthen Dennis's case for a US visa. The idea of traveling to Turkey first, followed by Spain, felt like a fresh beginning. It was a chance for us to reset and refocus on our goals. Despite everything that had happened with Seraphina and the difficult emotional toll it had taken on our circle, Dennis's resilience was an inspiration. He hadn't let one setback derail his dreams. Instead, he took it in stride, adapting to the situation and pushing forward with a renewed sense of determination.

At first, I wasn't sure if I was fully on board with Dennis's plan. After all, the idea of traveling to Turkey and Spain wasn't what we had originally envisioned. But somehow, it felt like the universe had a different path in store for us, and even though the road wasn't exactly what I had planned, it was still leading to something meaningful. God seemed to guide Dennis and me through the uncertainty, and in the process, I discovered more about myself and about the world than I could have ever expected.

As we traveled through Europe, exploring new places and learning more about different cultures, I realized that sometimes life's detours lead to the most unexpected blessings. Dennis and I had planned this trip to meet a goal, but it turned into something far more rewarding than we anticipated. But the most incredible part of the journey was when I reconnected with an old friend from my college days. It had been twenty years since I had last spoken to Nerissa, my close friend from university. We had lost touch over the years, as life had pulled us in different directions, but our bond had never faded. We promised each other that someday, we would meet again, even if it took years. That "someday" finally came. Nerissa had moved to California in the United States, and after much planning and coordination, we were able to arrange to meet in Barcelona. The excitement I felt when I saw her for the first time after so many years was overwhelming.

As soon as I spotted her waiting for us at the hotel, all the tiredness from the long flight melted away. The years seemed to vanish in an instant. Nerissa hadn't changed much—her smile was as warm and genuine as ever, and we quickly fell into the rhythm of our old conversations. It felt as though no time had passed at all. But there was something new about Nerissa. She was six months pregnant with her first child, and the joy on her face was infectious. She looked radiant, her hands gently resting on her belly as she shared the news. There was so much catching up to do, so many memories to relive, but Nerissa also had a special request. With smiles in her eyes, she told Dennis and me that she wanted us to be the godparents of her baby boy. It was an honor I hadn't expected, and I could hardly contain my emotions. The promise of becoming godparents marked a new chapter in our friendship, one that was filled with love, responsibility, and the deep bond that time and distance had never been able to erase.

As we spent time together, reminiscing about the past and talking about the future, I couldn't help but feel overwhelmed by the happiness of the moment. The trip, which had started with so much uncertainty and frustration, had brought me back to a place of joy. Not only had I seen new places in Europe, but I had also reconnected with a dear friend—and in doing so, I found a sense of peace and fulfillment that I hadn't realized I was missing. Seeing Nerissa, hearing about her life in California, and knowing that we would be part of her child's life in a meaningful way filled me with a sense of purpose. The reunion was not just a reunion of two old friends—it was the beginning of a new chapter, a new bond between our families, and a reminder that sometimes life's most unexpected paths can lead to the most beautiful destinations.

I walked down the cobbled alleys of Barcelona with a heart full of gratitude. Way back August of 2023, I never would have imagined that I could visit Europe, especially with my disabilities and limited finances. But here I was, standing in the heart of one of the most vibrant cities in the world. It was a humbling experience, and as I looked around the famous Sagrada La Familia church , I couldn't help but marvel at the beauty of the place. I knew, deep down, that this was more than just a trip; it was proof that God's plans for us are greater than we can ever imagine. Even in my darkest moments, He had a way of showing me that dreams could come true, no matter the odds. We didn't just stop in Barcelona.

My journey continued in the company of wonderful friends, and together we made our way to Amsterdam, where we spent an unforgettable night. There, the beauty of the canals, the art museums, and the city's unique charm enchanted us all. But it was Paris, France, that truly took my breath away. I had always dreamt of seeing the Eiffel Tower with my own eyes, and when we finally stood beneath its towering structure, I was in awe. Its magnificence wasn't just in its size, but in the way it symbolized the power of human ingenuity and perseverance.

We then ventured to the Louvre, home to some of the world's most famous masterpieces. Walking through its grand halls, I felt like I had stepped into a living history book. It was surreal, knowing that I was standing in the presence of art and culture that had shaped civilizations. That evening, we dined at a luxury floating restaurant along the Seine River. As we drifted past Paris' illuminated bridges, I couldn't help but feel like I was living in a dream. One of the most moving parts of our journey was when we visited the Notre-Dame Cathedral. The history and beauty of the church were overwhelming, but what made it even more special was the quiet moment I shared with my friend, Nerissa.

As we walked along the grand facade, we stopped to say a prayer together. Our hopes and wishes were simple yet profound: we prayed that we would somehow meet again in America. At the time, it felt like such an impossible dream. I was blind, and the reality of traveling to the United States seemed like an insurmountable obstacle. There was also the question of visas, which felt like a daunting barrier. I couldn't help but doubt myself—after all, my friend Dennis had been refused a U.S. visa not long before. If it could happen to him, why not me? But despite the uncertainty, something inside me refused to give up. I held on to the faith that God's plans were bigger than my doubts. I knew that the same God who had made this journey to Europe possible could open doors that I couldn't even see yet. So, I continued to walk forward, each step filled with hope and gratitude for all that I had already experienced, and all that was yet to come.

After our unforgettable time in Paris, we flew straight to Rome, Italy, and I was once again awestruck by the beauty of the world and the glory of God. The moment I stepped into Saint Peter's Square in Vatican City, I felt a sense of reverence that I can still hardly put into words. It was as if I had entered a sacred space that transcended time itself. I thought I was dreaming. The grandeur of the square, the towering columns, the fountains—it all felt so surreal, yet it was so real. I reached out and touched the cobblestones that surrounded the square, the very stones that countless pilgrims had walked on throughout history. It was a deeply humbling experience, and in that moment, I felt the presence of God in a way I never had before. Our journey didn't end there. We traveled to Assisi, a place that felt like a living testament to God's miracles.

There, I stood before the tomb of Saint Clare, a woman whose faith had inspired so many. When we entered the tomb, I could almost feel the weight of her legacy. It was overwhelming, the sense of holiness that filled the air. Then, we visited the tomb of Blessed Carlo Acutis , where I was reminded of God's infinite love and the miracles He still works in the world. I couldn't help but marvel at how God's power continues to manifest in ways beyond our understanding. And at that moment, as I stood before those sacred places, I found myself filled with a deep, quiet hope. If God could work such miracles for others, then why not for me? I found myself praying with a renewed sense of faith—believing that one day, my vision might be restored, that my sight could be made whole again. If He could heal the blind, then surely He could restore mine. It was a powerful thought, one that stayed with me as we continued our travels.

After a few days of exploring the treasures of Rome and the spiritual wonders of Assisi, we took a scenic train ride through the heart of Italy, heading toward Venice. The city of canals was every bit as magical as I had imagined. We glided through its narrow waterways, passing beneath charming bridges and along grand palaces, all while feeling the pulse of this ancient city beneath our feet. Venice was a place where history and beauty came alive, and I couldn't help but feel a deep sense of wonder at the sight of it all. From Venice, we journeyed onward to Milan, where we had a chance to explore the fashion capital of the world. Milan was vibrant and full of energy, a stark contrast to the quiet spirituality of Assisi, but equally captivating in its own way. The modern streets lined with designer boutiques were a sight to see, but what struck me most was the incredible Cathedral of Milan. The Gothic architecture, the intricate details—it was like stepping into another time. I marveled at the faith and creativity that had gone into building such a monumental structure, and it reminded me once again of the beauty that comes when human hands collaborate with divine inspiration.

Our second to the final destination was Zurich Switzerland, where we spent three days immersed in the stunning landscapes of the Alps. The air was crisp and fresh, and the snow-capped mountains stretched as far as the eye could see. The serene beauty of Switzerland was the perfect blend to our European journey. It was a time of quiet reflection, and I found myself contemplating how far I had come—not just in distance, but in my own personal journey of faith and growth.

Our European adventure culminated in London, England, where we spent five unforgettable days. London was everything I had imagined—its iconic landmarks like Big Ben and the Tower Bridge, the sprawling beauty of Hyde Park, and the timeless elegance of Buckingham Palace. But amidst all the sightseeing and excitement, there was a deeper, more personal reason why this final leg of the journey was so significant to me.

At that point, I was filled with a mix of gratitude and inner conflict. I had made it all the way to England, defying the odds that had once seemed insurmountable. I had traveled through countries I'd only dreamed of visiting, walked in places I never thought I'd set foot in. It was a moment of triumph, a victory over the limitations that had always tried to define me. But despite the wonder of it all, a part of me felt incomplete. I had longed to reach out to my Aunt Leoni, to share my achievement with her, to show her that despite my disabilities, despite the struggles I had faced, I had made it to England. It was more than just about the trip—it was about proving something to her, and perhaps, to myself. I called her and asked if we could visit. But for reasons I didn't fully understand, she refused. I was hurt, but at the same time, I couldn't deny the pride that swelled within me. I had made it to England. I wanted to show her that despite my limitations, I had done something she might never have expected. I wanted to demonstrate that I was more than what the world saw in me, more than just my disability, more than just the challenges that had always seemed to hold me back.

But the truth was, my pride and ego were standing in the way of something deeper. I had spent years feeling overlooked, misunderstood, and rejected by certain people—some of them even family. I wanted to prove I was someone worth recognizing, but in doing so, I realized I was still carrying a lot of pain. The disappointment of not being able to meet my aunt and share this moment with her was sharp, but it was compounded by the old wounds of rejection and discrimination I had suffered from others. Despite the incredible places I had seen, the miraculous way in which this journey had unfolded, part of me was still weighed down by the scars of my past. The faces of those who had looked at me with pity or disdain, the words of those who had belittled me because of my blindness and my limited means—those memories still lingered in my mind. They were like shadows, following me wherever I went.

At that moment, I had a choice. I could let that pain consume me, or I could embrace the miracle that God had given me. I was in London. I had stood on the streets of one of the greatest cities in the world, alongside people who loved and supported me. And that, in itself, was a victory. I had traveled across Europe—something I once thought impossible—and I had experienced the kind of beauty and wonder that dreams are made of. God had given me this incredible gift of travel, and in the midst of all the beauty I had witnessed, I realized that He had also given me the opportunity to heal. The journey was not just about the places I had visited, but about the way it had changed me inside. So, as I stood there in London, with all the wonder of the world around me, I let go of my pride and pain. I reminded myself that my worth was not defined by the approval of others or by the scars of the past. It was in the strength to move forward, to embrace the gifts I had been given, and to trust that my story wasn't over yet. There was still so much more to come.

As we landed back in Dubai, the feeling of accomplishment and gratitude still lingered in my heart. Dennis and I were already planning the next big celebration—our seventh anniversary of Jetliner Express, a milestone that seemed almost too good to be true. We had worked so hard to build this business, and now it was thriving. To mark this special occasion, we decided to celebrate in style, hosting an anniversary event in Batam, Indonesia, and then moving on to Singapore. The excitement wasn't just about the business. We were going to share this moment with the people who had been part of our journey from the very beginning—our office staff, our business partners, and most importantly, my parents and my brother Daniel. I couldn't wait to see their faces, to have them there with us as we celebrated this achievement together. It was a chance to show them how far we'd come, and it felt like the perfect way to honor their unwavering support and love over the years. But there was another dream I had—one that had been on my heart for a long time.

After our celebrations in Singapore and Batam, I decided to stay in the Philippines for three months. It was an opportunity to spend quality time with my parents in a way I hadn't been able to before and to reconcile our conflicts with my sister Caryl. Taking them abroad, showing them the world beyond the Philippines, was something I had always wanted to do, and now, with God's blessing, it was finally happening. It felt like a gift—a reward for the years of hard work, and a way to give back to the people who had sacrificed so much for me.

A few days before our trip to Singapore, Dennis invited Marshie to dinner. It was a special evening, as Marshie had just shared some significant news with us—she had decided to resign from her job and was preparing to stay in the United States for a longer period of time. Marshie was searching for new opportunities, but more than that, she was hoping to start a new chapter in her life, perhaps even find someone to build a family with. The excitement and uncertainty of such a decision were palpable, and as we sat down to enjoy a delicious meal at a Korean restaurant in Burjuman Mall, the conversation naturally turned to our own dreams and future plans. Marshie asked if Dennis and I had ever considered pursuing opportunities in Canada or the United States. It was a question I had pondered before but had never seriously entertained—until that moment. Marshie, always thoughtful and supportive, shared her own plans and gave us valuable advice on how to navigate the immigration process. I listened closely, absorbing every word of her recommendations. I shared with her that Dennis and I had an existing application to Canada and I also had an appointment at the U.S. Embassy in Manila scheduled for December 11, and while I was grateful for the chance, I also admitted to them my deep fear of rejection. The thought of going through an intense interview process, only to be turned away, terrified me. I was afraid of the disappointment and embarrassment that might follow. Dennis, ever the optimist, reassured me. "If it's for you, it's for you," he said, with a gentle smile. "And if it's not, then maybe God has something else in mind for you. Either way, you're not alone in this." His words, though simple, were deeply comforting. Marshie, too, encouraged me, reminding me that every opportunity, every challenge, was part of a bigger plan, one that might not always make sense in the moment but would reveal itself in time. Their encouragement sparked a shift in my mindset. I had been afraid of failing, of not being "enough." But as Marshie outlined the steps I needed to take for the U.S. visa process, I began to realize that, regardless of the outcome, pursuing this opportunity was worth it. The fear of rejection no longer seemed as daunting, not with the unwavering support of Dennis and Marshie. I knew that even if I didn't succeed, I would have learned and grown from the experience. Sometimes, the pursuit itself is as valuable as the destination.

Before the night came to a close, Marshie offered a heartfelt prayer for the three of us. She prayed that our dreams of living in Canada or the United States would one day become a reality, but more importantly, that we would have the courage to pursue those dreams no matter where they led us. Her prayer was simple yet powerful, filled with hope and belief that our futures were in God's hands, and that He would guide us to where we were meant to be. As we parted ways that evening, I felt a sense of peace I hadn't felt before. The uncertainty of the future still lingered, but it no longer seemed as intimidating. I had the support of people who believed in me, and I was ready to take the next step, trusting that whatever happened, it was all part of a greater plan. I carried Marshie's prayer with me, a reminder that even when the road ahead seemed unclear, we were not walking it alone.

During our time in Singapore and Indonesia , we visited some of the country's most stunning tourist spots—beautiful beaches of Batam, historical landmarks, and bustling cities. Each new place was a reminder of how blessed I was to be able to share these experiences with my family. But as beautiful as those places were, the most memorable part of our trip came unexpectedly, during our visit to Singapore. It was there that I reconnected with Ed, a dear friend I hadn't seen in years. She was accompanied by her friend Joy, and when we met, it felt like no time had passed at all. The joy and warmth that filled that moment were indescribable. I had missed Ed dearly, and to see her again, to hug her and catch up, was a gift I hadn't expected. It was a moment of pure happiness, and at that instant, I realized how much these connections—whether through business, family, or friendships—meant to me. They were the true treasures of life.

Being in that moment, surrounded by the people I loved and who loved me, I couldn't help but feel overwhelmingly grateful. The years of struggle, the challenges I'd faced, had all led to this. It wasn't just about the places I'd visited or the successes I had achieved—it was about the relationships, the love, and the moments of joy that made everything worthwhile. God had blessed me in so many ways, and this trip, this time with my family and friends, was a reminder that the best parts of life are often the simplest: love, connection, and the gift of sharing experiences with those who matter most.

CHAPTER 8

THE PROMISE

The time had come for our paths to diverge. Dennis had to return to Dubai for work commitments, while I, along with my family, business partners, and staff, needed to head back to Cebu. It was an early morning when we arrived at Changi International Airport, the quiet hum of the airport contrasting with the rush of emotions inside me. After a short while, we boarded our flight, and by 5:30 AM, the plane was ascending into the sky. As we crossed the clouds and soared to an altitude of 32,000 feet, my thoughts began to wander, a mix of gratitude for the journey I had just experienced and the looming uncertainty of what awaited me back in the Philippines. The hum of the airplane's engines seemed to lull me into deep contemplation.

For the first time in a long while, I allowed myself to fully reflect on what happened five years ago. I had made the decision to return to the Philippines with a clear goal: to find a surgeon who could help me regain my vision. It felt like the next logical step—an opportunity to take control of my future and reclaim what I had lost. But as I thought about the road ahead, I quickly realized that it wouldn't be an easy journey. I had been down similar paths before, hoping for a solution that would bring me clarity and healing, but each time, I had faced one obstacle after another. It wasn't that I had given up hope entirely, but I had grown weary of the fight. The roadblocks, the disappointments—they had tested my faith in ways I never expected. The anxiety, the self-doubt, and the fear of failure crept in, clouding my thoughts before. I had been down this path before—fighting for something I believed in, only to be met with disappointment. The pain of feeling unseen and unheard, of constantly battling against my limitations, had left me vulnerable.

And soon, what had started as anxiety turned into something deeper. I found myself sinking into a dark place, a place where thoughts of despair began to overshadow the light. The emotional toll had been heavy, and I was exhausted from the constant internal struggle. In the quiet of that plane, I found myself asking questions I couldn't answer: "*What would the next three months in Cebu hold for me? Would they bring a sense of renewal, a glimpse of hope, or would they be another chapter of sadness and frustration?"* The uncertainty was suffocating. My mind spiraled, imagining all the ways in which things could go wrong. It wasn't just fear; it was a deep sense of loss—a fear that maybe things would never change, that I would always be trapped in this cycle of longing and disappointment.

The turbulence inside me mirrored the physical turbulence of the flight. My thoughts became clouded with doubt, and at times, the weight of it all felt unbearable. I couldn't help but wonder if my journey, no matter how much I fought for it, was destined for failure. The question lingered in my mind: *What if I was never meant to regain my sight?* It was in that moment, as I sat there in the silence of the airplane, that I felt the crushing weight of my own limitations. I realized that my journey back to Cebu wasn't just about seeking medical help—it was also about facing the inner battle I had been avoiding for so long. The battle between hope and despair, between faith and fear, between the belief that I could overcome it all and the reality that the path ahead might be harder than I ever imagined. But even in that deep moment of darkness, I found a flicker of something—a quiet voice deep inside me, whispering that this, too, was part of the journey. That faith wasn't just about the victories, the moments of triumph. It was also about pushing through the pain, the doubt, and the fear, and trusting that God was with me, even in the darkest moments. I couldn't deny the pain I was feeling, nor could I

ignore the very real weight of my struggles, but I knew deep down that I wasn't alone. And somehow, that thought gave me the smallest measure of peace.

As I sat there on the plane, my mind tangled in anxiety and uncertainty, I suddenly drifted into a deep sleep. The turbulence outside seemed to mirror the chaos in my heart, but at that moment, I was transported into a dream that would stay with me forever. In the dream, I found myself walking down a dark, empty corridor. The silence was overwhelming, and I felt a sense of isolation, as if I were walking through a void. The air around me was thick, and my footsteps echoed in the emptiness. I wasn't sure where I was going or what I was looking for, but I felt a pull, an inexplicable sense of direction that led me forward.

As I reached the center of the room, I saw a cabinet standing alone in the middle of the space. The darkness seemed to recede around it, as though it were the only thing that existed in that place. My eyes locked onto the cabinet's door, where a paper was affixed. The words were bold and clear, as though they were meant for me to read: ***"For I know the plans I have for you," declares the Lord. "Plans to prosper you and not to harm you, plans to give you a hope and a future."*** The verse, though familiar, struck me with a force I hadn't anticipated. It was as if the words were speaking directly to the deepest part of my soul, reminding me of something I had forgotten in the midst of my struggles. *"Plans to prosper you… not to harm you… plans to give you hope and a future."* The weight of those words hung in the air, and at that moment, I felt a sudden shift.

The darkness around me seemed to lighten, and though I was still in that empty space, there was a new sense of direction—a quiet assurance that I was not alone, that there was a purpose even in the confusion and pain. Just as I began to process the meaning of those words, the plane jolted with turbulence, and I woke up with a start. My heart raced, but instead of fear, there was a strange calmness that settled over me. It was as though the dream had left a residue of peace in my heart, reminding me of something greater than my current struggles.

I reached for the window, my hand shaking slightly as I pulled open the shade. The bright sunlight flooded through, striking my face and my eyes, and for the first time in what felt like ages, I didn't recoil from it. The light felt warm, welcoming, almost like a sign. I closed my eyes for a moment, letting the sunlight bathe my face, and a feeling of hope stirred within me.

In that instant, I knew that despite all the challenges I had faced, despite the doubts and the fears that seemed to weigh me down, there was still a future waiting for me—one full of possibilities, even if I couldn't see it clearly just yet. The verse from my dream echoed in my mind again: *"Plans to prosper you… not to harm you… plans to give you hope and a future."* As I sat there, the turbulence that had once unsettled me no longer seemed so frightening. It was as though the dream had reminded me that even in the most uncertain of moments, God's plans were still unfolding. I might not understand all the details yet, but I knew that I wasn't walking this path alone. The sun shine brighter through the plane's window, and for the first time in a long while, I felt the stirrings of hope again. The journey was far from over, but I knew that I could face whatever came next with a renewed sense of purpose, knowing that God's plan for me was far greater than I could imagine. As the plane continued its journey through the skies, I made a quiet promise to myself. No matter what came next, I would face it with the courage to keep moving forward. The path ahead was uncertain, yes, but there was still hope. And hope, I knew, was something worth holding on to.

After a long and eventful journey, we finally arrived safely in Cebu. The familiar sights of the city brought a sense of relief, and as we made our way to our house in Liloan, I couldn't help but feel a deep sense of gratitude. Walking through the door, I was greeted warmly by our employees, who had gathered to welcome me back. Their smiles and friendly words made me realize how much I had missed the simple comforts of home.

Later that evening, my sister Caryl and her family came to visit. It had been too long since we had spent time together, and the reunion felt like a balm to my soul. We gathered around the dinner table, sharing stories, laughter, and meals, just like old times. The warmth of my family's presence filled the room, and for the first time in what felt like ages, I felt truly at peace. The weight of my struggles and the uncertainties I had been carrying began to lift, if only for a moment, as I basked in the love and connection that surrounded me.

During dinner, I shared with them my upcoming plans for the U.S. visa interview in Manila, scheduled for December. I could sense the excitement in the air as I told them about the opportunity, though I also admitted the lingering doubts I had about the process. But my family, as always, was there to lift my spirits. My sister Caryl and my brother-in-law Jeff were eager to support me, and Jaira and Chloe, my niece and nephew, were both excited about the trip.

The thought of having them by my side in Manila during the interview brought a sense of comfort. Their presence would remind me that no matter what happened, I wasn't facing this challenge alone. We made plans to stay in Manila for four days—just enough time to attend the interview, but also to reconnect with old friends, visit relatives, and explore the city. One of the highlights of the trip, which had everyone excited, was our plan to visit Skyranch, the famous theme park in Tagaytay. The idea of spending a day together, laughing, riding roller coasters, and making new memories, was something we all looked forward to.

For a brief moment, it felt like all the weight of the world was lifted off my shoulders, replaced by the simple joy of spending time with the people who meant the most to me. That night, as I lay in bed thinking about the coming days, I couldn't help but feel a sense of anticipation. There was so much to look forward to—seeing old friends, exploring new places, and sharing precious moments with family. My heart was full, not just with hope, but with the understanding that family would always be my anchor, my source of strength, no matter what happened with the visa interview or anything else that lay ahead.

During my stay in Cebu, there were still moments when the shadows of my past struggles would resurface. Sleepless nights became a familiar companion, as memories of my darkest hour—when I had battled with my own mind and spirit—came flooding back. It was a time when fear, doubt, and anxiety seemed to have the upper hand. The weight of it all felt unbearable at times, and I often questioned how I could keep moving forward. But in those quiet, restless hours, I clung to the promise I had made to myself: that God's plans for me were greater than my own. I reminded myself that He would never leave me, no matter how fierce the battle felt. The darkness might return, but His light would guide me through. I held tightly to this belief, even when everything around me seemed uncertain.

And as the days passed, the assurance that I was not alone slowly began to heal the wounds of my soul. When the time finally came to fly to Manila, I felt a mix of excitement and anxiety. I wasn't sure what to expect from the US Embassy interview, but I was determined to approach it with faith. We checked into a hotel right across from the embassy, and the location felt oddly comforting, like a sign that everything was falling into place. It felt like I was on the cusp of something important, but also at peace with whatever the outcome would be. This wasn't just about the visa interview; it was about the journey, about trusting God's plan for me.

The next day, we took the opportunity to visit Jeff's hometown and meet his mother, Emelita. She greeted us warmly and prepared a delicious meal, and I could see the love and pride she had for her family. Her kindness and hospitality gave me a sense of calm, like a reminder that even in the midst of challenges, there was still beauty in the small moments of connection and care. We all decided to make the most of the trip and take a detour to Tagaytay for a day of relaxation and exploration.

As we drove through the city, the excitement was palpable—especially for Jaira and Chloe, who could hardly contain their joy. Our first stop was the iconic Picnic Grove, where we strolled around, taking in the cool air and lush surroundings. Then we made our way to the Palace in the Sky, a historical site with breathtaking views of the Taal Volcano and its lake. The sight was nothing short of magnificent, and I could see the awe in my nieces' eyes as they gazed at the landscape. But the best was yet to come. The highlight of the day was our visit to Skyranch, the famous theme park in Tagaytay. Jaira and Chloe were beside themselves with excitement as we entered the park. The thrilling rides, the panoramic views of Taal, and the laughter we shared as a family made it a day we would never forget. The girls were especially thrilled by the Ferris wheel, which offered a bird's-eye view of the sprawling landscape, and I could hear their infectious laughter from across the park. It wasn't just the rides that made it memorable—it was the sense of togetherness, of being a family united in joy, that filled my heart. It was a perfect day, one filled with wonder, laughter, and precious memories. For me, it was also the first time that we all traveled together as one family, and that fact alone made it even more special. In a way, the joy of being surrounded by loved ones helped to heal the lingering fears and doubts I had carried with me for so long. The warmth of their presence reminded me that, no matter what happened with the visa interview, I was not alone. That day in Tagaytay was more than just an adventure—it was a reminder that, even in the darkest moments of life, there are days of joy waiting for us, days when we are blessed to be surrounded by those who love us. And in that joy, there is healing, hope, and the strength to keep moving forward.

On our third day in Manila, Sunday, December 10, I felt a deep desire to connect with God in a way that I hadn't in a while. I approached my mother, my sister, and my brother-in-law Jeff, asking if they would be willing to join me for a church service at Every Nation in Fort Bonifacio, Taguig City. I wasn't sure what they would think, but they all agreed to come with me, and I felt a sense of peace knowing that we would be together for this special time. We arrived at The Christians Church just before the 10:00 AM service began. As I walked through the doors of the church, I felt a familiar warmth, a sense of comfort in the midst of all the uncertainty that had been weighing on me. It reminded me of the years I spent working in Makati City, where I sometimes attended church services—though, admittedly, not as consistently as I would have liked.

Back then, life had been a blur of meetings and deadlines, and I often found it difficult to make time for worship. But today, in the quiet of that church, I felt a strong pull to reconnect, to make space for God in my heart again. As the service began, the worship songs filled the air, and the pastor took the stage. His words resonated deeply with me. I remember he spoke about the power of prayer and trusting God with our deepest desires and struggles. He encouraged the congregation to pray with boldness, knowing that God hears our hearts and responds in His perfect timing. As I sat there, listening to the pastor's message, I felt a quiet stirring in my spirit. I knew it was time to offer my own prayers—prayers that I had been holding in my heart for a long time. I closed my eyes for a moment and began to speak to God, silently listing the things that weighed most heavily on me.

First, I prayed for my vision. The inability to see clearly had been a constant challenge, and I longed to regain my sight—to see the world as I once had and not through a haze of uncertainty.

Second, I prayed for the health of my family. I asked God to protect them, to keep them strong and healthy, and to surround them with peace and love. Their well-being was my greatest concern, and I wanted nothing more than to see them thrive.

Lastly, I prayed for confidence during my upcoming US visa interview. The fear of rejection weighed on me, and I wasn't sure if I had the strength to face the interview with the poise I needed. I asked God to give me the self-assurance I lacked, to guide my words and actions, and to help me remain calm and composed.

Above all, I prayed that whatever the outcome of the interview, His will would be done. If I was meant to pass, I trusted that He would open that door. If not, I knew there was a greater purpose at work, and I would find peace in that as well. As I offered these prayers, I felt a deep sense of peace begin to settle in my heart. It wasn't the peace that comes from having all the answers, but the peace that comes from surrendering everything to God's hands. I didn't know what the future held, but I knew that I wasn't walking this journey alone. The service continued, but my mind remained focused on those three prayers. I felt a quiet assurance in my spirit—an assurance that, no matter what happened in the coming days, God was already at work in ways I couldn't yet see. All I had to do was trust Him and have faith in His plan. After the two-hour service at the Church, we decided to drive straight to Antipolo, to visit the famous Antipolo Church and its shrine, as per the request of Jeff's mother, Emelita. As we made our way to the church, I couldn't help but feel a quiet sense of gratitude wash over me. The day had already been filled with so much joy, peace, and spiritual reflection, and this next stop felt like a continuation of the blessings that had been unfolding. As we entered the church grounds and walked toward the shrine, I was overcome by a rush of nostalgia. The peaceful surroundings of Antipolo brought back memories of my childhood, when my sister and I would walk the streets of the city with our mother. I could almost hear the soft chatter of our steps as we strolled together, and the image of my mother carrying a basket of rice cakes—a local treat we would enjoy as we walked—came flooding back to me. The simplicity of those moments, the sense of warmth and belonging, was something I hadn't thought about in years. But as I stood there, in the quiet of the Antipolo shrine, I felt like those memories were reaching out to me, reminding me of the love and bond we had as a family.

The visit to the shrine was peaceful, a moment of reflection and prayer. We lit candles and offered our own quiet prayers of thanks and hope. I prayed for continued healing, for my vision to be restored, and for the strength to face whatever challenges lay ahead. I also thanked God for bringing my family together in this way—for the opportunity to travel and experience these moments of connection, for the opportunity to deepen our relationships and create new memories. As we sat and ate the rice cakes, reminiscing about the past and talking about the future, I couldn't help but feel an overwhelming sense of happiness.

The simplicity of the day, the shared moments of laughter and conversation, reminded me of the importance of family. This trip to Manila, this time spent with my mother, sister, and Jeff, was more than just a visit for the US visa interview—it was a gift of reconciliation, of healing, and of rebuilding relationships that had been distant for so long. I felt truly blessed. The trip had already brought so many unexpected gifts—peace, laughter, connection—and the healing of old wounds. There was a new kind of relationship forming between us, one built on mutual understanding, love, and respect. It wasn't just about being together physically; it was about reconnecting on a deeper, more meaningful level.

As we left Antipolo and Muntinlupa and made our way back to our hotel, I felt a deep sense of fulfillment in my heart. The day had been filled with so much happiness, and I knew that, no matter what happened next—whether I passed the visa interview or not—the true blessing of this trip had been the restoration of family bonds and the joy of being together. Today was the day—the moment of truth that I had been preparing for. I woke up early, around 4:00 AM, feeling a mixture of anticipation and calm. The weight of what was about to happen hung in the air, but I felt ready. I had no choice but to trust in the process and, more importantly, trust in God's plan.

I got ready quietly, careful not to rush, and made my way to meet my brother-in-law Jeff, who would be accompanying me to the US Embassy. He had been a steady source of support throughout this journey, and having him by my side gave me a sense of comfort as I faced this important moment. We arrived at the embassy well before my appointment time, which was scheduled for 7:00 AM.

As we entered the embassy, the weight of the situation felt real, but I didn't allow myself to become overwhelmed. I had already prayed, and I knew that God had a plan for me, whether this was the right time or not. It was in His hands. The process inside the embassy was long, as expected—appointments, document clarifications, biometrics—but I stayed focused and calm throughout each step. As I moved through the various stages, I couldn't help but reflect on how far I had come, from the uncertainty about my vision to the fears about my worthiness of passing the visa interview. Every step felt like a victory in itself. The more I moved through the process, the more confident I became, not in my own abilities, but in the fact that God was with me every step of the way.

Finally, after what felt like hours, I reached the window where I would face the consul. This was the moment that had filled me with anxiety and doubt in the past, but today, there was only peace. I stood there, waiting, and when the officer asked me about the purpose of my trip to the United States, I felt a surge of confidence. I explained my objectives clearly and concisely: I would be visiting, taking part in a brief itinerary, and had the necessary ties back home to show that I wasn't intending to overstay. Surprisingly, the officer didn't ask many more questions. It was a brief, one-minute conversation, and the officer said " Congratulations! Your visa is approved." There was no long wait, no further interrogation, just the simple, clear answer I had been praying for. I couldn't believe it. My mind raced as I walked away from the window, the weight of the moment settling in. I had passed the most difficult visa application process, something that had once seemed impossible, but with God's guidance, it had all worked out. I had walked into that embassy with uncertainty and fear, but I left with a deep sense of gratitude and awe at how God had worked in such mysterious ways. It wasn't just the visa that was a gift; it was the reminder that, when we trust in God's timing, even the most daunting obstacles can be overcome. As Jeff and I left the embassy, I couldn't stop smiling. The joy I felt wasn't just for the approval—it was for the journey itself, the lessons I had learned along the way, and the faith that had carried me through.

As we stepped back into the hotel after the thrilling news of my visa approval, a wave of relief and joy washed over me. It was a victory we couldn't help but celebrate, not just for the visa itself, but for everything this journey had represented. We had faced so many hurdles along the way—both external and internal—but here we were, having made it through. We had arrived at this moment together, stronger and more connected than ever. To mark this momentous occasion, my family and I decided to visit my hometown in Laguna. It had been many years since I had returned to this place, where I spent the first twenty years of my life. The familiar sights of the town brought back memories—of my childhood, the simpler days, and the people who had shaped me. We went to a hot spring resort in the area, a place where I had spent countless hours growing up. The warm waters seemed to mirror the sense of healing that had taken place in my heart over the past few weeks—healing not just for my body but for my spirit.

After spending some time at the resort, we took a short drive to our old house in Cabuyao, where my family and I had lived for so long. Seeing the house again, though much changed, stirred a deep sense of nostalgia. It was where so many of my formative memories were made—the place where my siblings and I had laughed, fought, and grown up together.

Now, standing there again, it felt like a full circle, a reminder of how far I had come on my journey, both physically and emotionally. Though the trip was short, it was meaningful in ways I hadn't expected. It wasn't just about the visa or the approval—it was about reconnecting with my roots, rebuilding bonds with my family, and rediscovering parts of myself that had been lost over time. It was about understanding that no matter how far we may go or how much we change, our roots remain with us, and they shape the people we become.

A week later, I received my passport with the US visa stamp securely inside. Holding it in my hands was surreal—almost too good to be true. It felt like a dream realized, but it was also a confirmation of something deeper. This trip to the Philippines, this whole journey, had been about more than just paperwork and processes. It had been a journey of personal growth, spiritual awakening, and reconnecting with the people I love. The bond with my siblings had strengthened, and the family connections had deepened in ways I didn't expect. I had received my US visa without too many difficulties, yes, but the true blessing lay in the relationships that had been healed, the love that had been rekindled, and the peace that had been restored. As I reflected on the experience, I realized that the victory was not just about a stamp in my passport. It was about the journey—how God had worked in mysterious ways, leading me through challenges and triumphs, and bringing me closer to my family, to my roots, and ultimately, to a deeper understanding of myself.

After spending several months in the Philippines, reconnecting with my family and reflecting on all that I had been through, I returned to Dubai just after the New Year. It felt like stepping back into a familiar rhythm—managing my business online, taking care of household chores, and trying to find some normalcy again after such a transformative year. Despite the comfort of routine, there was a part of me that couldn't quite shake the sense of change that had settled within me. As the months passed, I found myself reflecting more deeply on the blessings and lessons of the year before. I had turned 40, and though the milestone felt significant, I didn't feel any overwhelming sense of dread or anxiety about aging. Instead, I felt grateful. Grateful for the gift of travel, for the healing of relationships, and for the opportunity to start fresh in so many ways. To celebrate, I decided to take a trip to Europe for the second time, this time with some of my closest friends, including Dennis.

We spent time in Santorini, Greece—a place I had always dreamed of visiting. As I stood on the edge of the island, leaning on the post of the grotto, watching the world-famous sunset paint the sky in shades of orange, pink, and purple, I felt overwhelmed by the beauty of the moment. It was a surreal experience, almost as though the world had stopped just for a moment to let me breathe in the magnificence of God's creation. I couldn't help but feel that this moment, this trip, was part of a larger plan that God had for me—a plan I still couldn't fully understand, but one that I trusted would unfold in time.

Returning back to Dubai, I found myself settling into my life again. But the next surprise came in the form of a visit from Seraphina—someone who, for all intents and purposes, had faded out of my life after our fall-out. It had been a year since we'd last spoken, and I had long resigned myself to the idea that we might never reconnect. So when she walked through the door of our apartment, my heart was filled with a mixture of surprise, caution, and curiosity. Seraphina explained that she had been through a lot in the past year. After so many months of silence, she shared with me the deeply painful news that her father was in the terminal stage of lung cancer. Her voice cracked as she spoke of the heartbreak she was facing, and I could hear the sadness in her words, a sadness that went far beyond just the weight of her father's illness. She seemed lost, as though the weight of her grief had overwhelmed her to the point where she didn't know how to navigate the world anymore. My heart went out to her. Despite a year of silence, despite the painful history between us, I couldn't turn my back on her at this moment. I felt a deep sense of compassion for what she was going through. It was impossible not to, especially knowing how fleeting life could be. I offered her a listening ear, a shoulder to lean on, and most importantly, I reminded her that even in the darkest times, God's grace was there to carry us through. It was a complicated moment—filled with both regret for the lost time between us and empathy for her pain. I didn't know what would come of this reconnection, or where it would lead, but I knew that the compassion and forgiveness I had been learning to embrace in my own life would be the key to whatever healing might come from this.

A few days after Seraphina's visit, she returned, this time bringing Kuri and Cristy with her. The reunion, though unexpected, was strangely comforting. It felt like a small circle was being reformed, one that had been broken by time, misunderstandings, and past hurts. They came into our apartment, and as we sat together, it quickly became clear that the conversation would not be about casual catch-ups or superficial pleasantries.

Instead, it was an honest exchange, one that carried the weight of unresolved emotions and the need for healing. They began sharing their side of the story, explaining the difficulties they had faced with Aline,

Sally, and Ruby. It was clear that there had been misunderstandings, miscommunications, and, at times, outright conflict between them. They spoke of their feelings—how they had been hurt, how they felt misunderstood or mistreated—and it was eye-opening to hear their perspective. It was a conversation that was long overdue, one that, in many ways, had been stifled by silence and distance. Listening to their stories, I couldn't help but reflect on how much pain people could carry, often without ever expressing it. As they spoke, I realized that the tensions they had been holding onto for so long were not just about the actions of others; they were also about their own hurt, their own longing for understanding and reconciliation. It reminded me that no one is perfect, and sometimes, the conflicts we experience in life are not just about what others do to us, but how we choose to respond, how we choose to heal.

In the midst of their stories, Seraphina continued to express her gratitude, especially towards Dennis. She spoke fondly of the genuine friendship he had offered to her and her family, a friendship that had been consistent and unwavering, even when they had nothing to offer in return. It was humbling to hear her acknowledge the kindness that Dennis had shown them, especially considering the challenges they had faced over the years. She often told us how much it meant to her, how important it was to know that there were people who, despite the ups and downs, were always ready to lend a hand. She spoke of the times when they had needed support—whether it was financial, emotional, or just someone to lean on—and how, in those moments, Dennis had been there for them. It wasn't just about the big gestures or the material things; it was about the unwavering presence, the genuine care that had been offered without strings attached.

As I listened to her, I felt a deep sense of gratitude for Dennis. His ability to offer such genuine friendship, even when others had fallen away, was a reminder of the kind of person he was—a person whose heart was open to others, whose commitment to kindness was not conditional on past mistakes or misunderstandings. In that moment, I realized how much healing had taken place, not just for Seraphina and her family, but for all of us. The time we spent together—those weeks of reconnecting, of sharing, of rebuilding—was a testament to the power of forgiveness and the importance of nurturing relationships, even when the road to healing is long and uncertain.

After my birthday and the emotional reconciliation with Seraphina, things seemed to be falling into place. I had spent time rebuilding relationships with Kuri and Tin, and there was a sense of peace settling in my heart. It was as if I was finding my place again—both in the world and in my own life. But as life often does, just when things felt stable, a curveball came my way. I received a letter regarding my application for Canada. My heart sank as I read the words "Application Refused"—the disappointment was palpable. I had worked so hard, hoped so much, and yet, it felt like the door had closed.

But surprisingly, this time, I didn't feel the same crushing weight of failure that I had experienced with earlier rejections. Instead, I took a deep breath and reminded myself that not every door that closes is meant to keep us out forever. Sometimes, it's just a momentary setback—a part of the journey. What I didn't expect was the twist that came next. Dennis, who had faced a similar visa rejection earlier, had just received approval for his US visa. His approval was a victory not just for him, but for both of us. Now, both of us had US visas valid for ten years. I couldn't help but feel a sense of relief and joy that, despite the hurdles, we had reached this milestone together. A few weeks later, Marshie returned to Dubai from the United States, bringing with her a wealth of stories, experiences, and new hopes. She had been in the US for some time and had settled into her life there, but as soon as we met up, her energy and excitement were infectious. She had heard about our visa situation and was thrilled that Dennis and I had both secured our US visas. She was hopeful that, one day, we could all travel together.

Then, Marshie shared something that completely took me by surprise. Despite our initial rejection from Canada, she told us there was still a way we could go—by applying for the Canada Electronic Travel Authorization (eTA). She explained that even though our visa applications had been refused, we could still apply online for the eTA by presenting our valid US visas. The process was simple, and she assured us it would only take a few minutes. Skeptical yet hopeful, I followed her advice, submitting the application with my heart pounding in my chest. Less than fifteen minutes later, I received an email confirmation: We had been approved for a Canadian eTA. My heart soared with gratitude—I couldn't believe it. We had been granted the opportunity to visit Canada for up to five years with multiple entries. It felt like a miracle, like God had opened a door that had initially been shut in our faces.

At that moment, I couldn't help but marvel at how God's grace had worked in our lives. After the disappointment of the refusal letter, I had allowed myself to feel discouraged, but this new opportunity reminded me that God's plans for us are greater than anything we can imagine. Sometimes, when we think we've reached the end of the road, we find that the path we thought was closed is only leading us in a new direction, toward something even better than we had hoped for. With our eTAs approved, the three of us—Marshie, Dennis, and I—began making plans for a two-week visit to Canada. We decided on a trip that would start on June 14th and stretch until the end of the month. I couldn't contain my excitement. Not only was this a chance to explore a new country, but it also symbolized how far we had come—how much we had grown, how many hurdles we had overcome, and how much grace and favor had been poured into our lives.

Just before our scheduled flight to Toronto, Canada, the news that I never expected came—a call from Kuri that would change the course of our day. Seraphina and Vera"s father had passed away. The shock was immediate, and my heart sank with the weight of the news. Losing a loved one is never easy, and it struck me that, while we were preparing for new adventures, our friends were dealing with a deep loss. Without hesitation, Dennis and I made plans to go to Sharjah to offer our support. This wasn't just a visit; it was a chance for us to stand beside our friends during one of the most difficult moments in their lives.

We arrived at their house and immediately joined the family, offering what little comfort we could in a time of grief. We prayed together for the soul of their father, asking God to grant him eternal peace, and for strength and comfort to the family left behind. It felt like such a small thing to do, yet it was all we could offer—a prayer and our presence, standing in solidarity with them as they navigated the pain of their loss. The mood was somber, but there was also a sense of peace in the quiet moments of prayer, in the shared understanding that, even in grief, God's grace was present, offering solace to those who mourned. It reminded me of how important it is to be there for one another, to show up when it matters the most, without hesitation, without expecting anything in return. As we sat together,

Seraphina and Vera quietly pulled Dennis aside. They had a request that came with a heavy heart—one that was born from the need to act swiftly and with urgency. They needed to fly back to the Philippines for the funeral and the family's mourning rituals, but they didn't have the funds to purchase the tickets. The request was humbling, and I could see the struggle in their eyes as they asked for help. Without any hesitation, Dennis responded. He offered to assist them through our agency, providing the necessary funds for the flight tickets. There were no questions asked, no judgment passed—just a simple act of kindness, given freely. Dennis's response was a testament to the generosity of spirit that I had come to admire in him. He didn't hesitate to lend a hand, even when the situation was difficult and the emotions were high. He simply wanted to help, because that's who he is—a man who offers support when others need it the most.

As we left their house, I felt a deep sense of gratitude for the opportunity to be there for Seraphina and Vera during such a difficult time. I also felt a quiet pride in Dennis's ability to give without reservation. It wasn't about the money—it was about showing up for friends in their time of need, about offering compassion and love without expecting anything in return. It was another reminder of how God works through us to be a blessing to others, even in moments of loss.

On June 14th, we boarded a direct flight from Dubai to Toronto, Canada, with excitement buzzing in the air. The flight was long—almost sixteen hours on a massive plane, each hour stretching out, making my body weary and restless. Yet, amidst the exhaustion, there was something more powerful that kept me going: the sheer excitement of finally reaching my dream destination. For years, I had set my sights on visiting Canada. It was a long-term goal, one that seemed so far out of reach at times, especially with all the struggles I had faced—my blindness, the visa refusals, and personal challenges. But now, as the plane soared through the skies, I realized that it was finally happening. God had truly answered my prayers. Despite everything that had seemed impossible, He had made a way, reminding me that His promises never fail. I was living my dream—standing on the edge of a new chapter in a country I had always wanted to explore. We spent almost five days in Toronto, taking in the beauty of the city. It was everything I had hoped for—iconic landmarks, modern architecture, and bustling streets. We met new people, made new friends, and created memories that would last a lifetime. But the highlight, without a doubt, was visiting the majestic Niagara Falls. Standing there, in awe of the powerful rush of water cascading down, I couldn't help but reflect on how far I had come. The sight of the falls reminded me of life's ebb and flow—how sometimes we must go through the struggles to appreciate the beauty that lies ahead.

After our time in Toronto, we flew straight to Alberta. The flight was just over four hours, and as we landed in Calgary, I was filled with anticipation for the next leg of our journey. Marshie, who had already been in Canada for some time, was waiting for us at Calgary International Airport. Her smile was infectious, and it felt so good to hear a familiar voice in this new land. From the airport, she drove us to Banff, a picturesque town nestled in the Canadian Rockies. As we drove through the winding roads, surrounded by towering mountains and pristine lakes, I couldn't help but feel an overwhelming sense of gratitude. I had set foot in a place I had only ever dreamed of, and now, with friends by my side, I was seeing it with my own blurry eyes. This was a place where nature's beauty was boundless, and every moment felt like a blessing. Banff was more magnificent than I could have imagined, and with Marshie's guidance, I was able to appreciate its splendor even more.

As I walked toward the edge of the lake, I was enveloped by a sense of peace I had never known before. The crisp, cold breeze brushed against my skin, and for a brief moment, everything else fell away. It was just me, the lake, and the towering mountains surrounding me. The water was still, reflecting the clear blue sky above, and the quiet solitude of the moment felt almost sacred. In that stillness, I felt a sense of healing wash over me. It wasn't just the cool air or the beauty of the landscape—it was as if nature itself was speaking to me. I felt God's presence in a way that I couldn't explain, but I knew that He was reminding me that His plans are far greater than any of the problems I've faced. A wave of emotion swept through me as I stood there, gazing out over the calm waters. The weight of past struggles, the pain, the confusion, and the doubts I had carried with me seemed to lift, if only for a moment. I could almost feel the "ghost bombs"—those inner walls I'd built to protect myself—falling away, piece by piece. The healing was real, and I knew that in this moment, God was telling me that light always follows the darkness. No matter how difficult the journey had been, there was a future full of hope waiting for me. The sound of the wind rustling through the trees and the gentle lapping of the water against the shore seemed to whisper that life wasn't just about enduring the hard times. It was also about learning to see beyond them, to trust that, with faith, there was always a way through, always a path toward healing and growth. At that moment, I felt an overwhelming sense of gratitude—not just for the opportunity to be in Canada, not just for the breathtaking beauty of Banff, but for the journey itself. The two weeks we spent in Canada became a turning point for me, a milestone in my life where I could look back and see how far I'd come. It wasn't just a trip to a new country; it was a chance to renew my spirit, to be reminded that life is a series of moments, both light and dark, and that ultimately, it is the light that will guide us forward.

As we sat in the airport, waiting for our flight back to Dubai, my thoughts drifted back to a painful memory—my Aunt Liza. It had been a year since she passed away, and in that time, I had thought often of the regrets she left behind. One of the things she spoke of the most in her final days was her longing for reconciliation, particularly with my Aunt Leoni. The unresolved tension between them had weighed heavily on her heart, and in those last conversations, she expressed deep sorrow for the distance that had grown between them over the years. At that quiet moment, with the bustling sounds of the airport around me, I felt a tug at my heart.

Could I forgive? It wasn't just about Aunt Liza's regrets anymore; it was about my own heart and whether I could break the silence and bridge the gap between myself and my Aunt Leoni. I looked down at my phone, my fingers hesitating for just a moment. And then, almost without thinking, I dialed her number. "Can I forgive this person?" I asked myself one more time. And before I could question it further, my heart answered with a deep, unconditional compassion that I didn't know I was capable of. "How are you, Tita? I miss you," I said as soon as she picked up. There was a pause on the other end, and then her voice—soft, weary, and filled with a sadness I hadn't expected—spoke back. She had been living in England for decades, and while she had built a life there, the loneliness in her voice was unmistakable. It was as if time had worn her down in ways I hadn't realized, and though she had spent so many years away, it seemed that happiness still eluded her. We talked for a while—about life, about the years that had passed, about the things left unsaid between us. And then, in a moment of shared vulnerability, I asked her something I hadn't expected to say. "Tita, I want to ask for your forgiveness," I told her. "For the things I might have done or said, for the distance that grew between us. I'm sorry." She was quiet for a moment, and I could sense the weight of her own emotions, the grief of all those years spent apart. Then, with a voice softened by time, she answered. "I've been waiting for this, for so long," she said, her words full of the same sorrow that Aunt Liza had expressed before she passed. "I've carried this with me, and I'm sorry too." The moment was filled with so much more than just words—it was a long overdue healing. It felt like a burden lifting off both of our shoulders. There, in the hum of the airport, we were able to mend a piece of our past, and the relief that followed was palpable. It was as if, through that single conversation, we had taken a step toward something bigger than ourselves—a kind of peace that only God can bring. I realized, at that moment, that God truly can move mountains—even the hardest of hearts can soften. Even the most painful divides can be healed. And in my own heart, I felt an overwhelming sense of release, as if the tension that had always lingered was finally gone.

After the heartfelt conversation with my aunt Leony, we began staying in touch regularly, and our communication continued even after I returned to Dubai. It felt so comforting to have that ongoing connection, and looking back, I couldn't help but reflect on how special my first trip to Canada had been. The memories of that time are vivid, and they fill me with gratitude.

As I sat on the plane heading back to Dubai, my thoughts wandered to Roxanne, a dear friend who had been such a generous help with our travel insurance and also provided the insurance for our agency. I first met Roxanne back in 2015 when Dennis and I were invited to a Christian service. We instantly clicked, and over the years, we became good friends. She's now married to Carlo, another wonderful friend of mine, and they have two incredible sons, Caleb and Aeron. Dennis and I had been thinking of giving the boys a souvenir gift as a token of our appreciation for their family's kindness.

Upon arriving in Dubai, we immediately messaged Roxanne on WhatsApp to arrange a meet-up. We invited her and Carlo to come over to our apartment for dinner, and we were thrilled when she responded with such warmth and gratitude. However, she mentioned that they had a prior commitment: they would be attending church service on Saturday at 7:00 PM. As I read her message, something stirred inside me.

After the service, we invited Roxanne and her family to join us for dinner at Shakey's in Bur Juman. We were both looking forward to it, as it was the perfect way to extend the evening and spend more time with our friends. At exactly 9:00 PM, Dennis and I arrived at the restaurant, placed our order, and settled in. A few minutes later, Roxanne and her family walked in, radiating joy and excitement. There was a warmth in their presence that made the evening even more special. As we sat down at the table, the conversation naturally shifted to our recent trip to Canada. We shared stories of the beautiful sights, the friendly people, and the amazing experiences we had. But then Carlo, with his thoughtful curiosity, asked a question that caught me off guard: "How do you feel and appreciate the beauty of Canada, Clark?" For a moment, I was silent. The question, so simple yet so deep, took me to a place I hadn't expected to go. As I sat there, I reflected on what Canada means to me—not just as a destination, but as a reminder of how far I had come.

Finally, I spoke, my voice soft at first, then gaining strength as I shared my story. I began to tell them about the time I lost my sight due to retinal detachment. I described the terror and confusion that engulfed me, and how my world became dark and uncertain. I explained how I went back to the Philippines to undergo surgery, only for the operation to be unsuccessful. That's when the real struggle began. The physical pain was overwhelming, but it was the emotional toll that almost broke me. I found myself sinking into a deep well of anxiety and depression, unable to find a way out. There were nights when I couldn't see any reason to keep going, and I even attempted suicide. But I didn't stop there. I told them about the turning point in my life—the moment when I encountered Jesus Christ in my darkest hour. It wasn't an instant transformation, but bit by bit, He began to piece my life back together. I told them about the peace that slowly replaced my fears, and how my heart, once full of sorrow, began to open up to hope and healing. Roxanne, listening intently, seemed genuinely moved by my story. She smiled warmly, her eyes full of understanding. "I'm so happy to hear about your transformation, Clark," she said. "Your journey is inspiring. You should share it with others. Your story could give so many people hope." Her words resonated with me deeply.

It was something I had always wanted to do but never fully believed I could. I told her that, in fact, I had been thinking about writing a book—something to not only share my struggles but to inspire others who were facing their own battles. I wanted to give them the message that no matter how dark life gets, there is always a way out, and there is always hope. Roxanne's encouragement meant more to me than I could express. She promised to support me in this endeavor, offering not just her moral support but also her prayers for success. "I'll pray that your book will touch many hearts and help others," she said.

As we finished our meal, I couldn't help but feel a renewed sense of purpose. This dinner, this conversation—it wasn't just about catching up with friends. It felt like a pivotal moment, one that would stay with me for a long time. I realized that sharing my story wasn't just about healing myself—it was about helping others heal too. And with Roxanne's promise of support, I knew I wasn't walking this journey alone.

A week later, I found myself thinking about attending a Christian service. Since we had no prior commitments or plans for the day, the idea seemed to surface naturally. I asked myself, *"Why not attend the church service?"* It felt like the perfect opportunity to connect more deeply with Roxanne's family and to experience something meaningful together. I shared my thoughts with Dennis, and without hesitation, he agreed. It wasn't just about spending time with dear friends—it was an opportunity to reflect spiritually and gain a deeper sense of connection with one another. We were both excited.

That Saturday, we made our way to Holy Trinity Church for a Christ Commission Fellowship (CCF) service. When we met up with Roxanne and her family, I felt a sense of anticipation and peace wash over me. This wasn't going to be just another casual gathering—it felt like a shared experience, one that could bring us even closer together. The church, as we entered, was filled with warmth—not just from its inviting atmosphere but from the people who gathered there, all with open hearts and a common purpose. The service itself was beautiful, full of moments of reflection, joy, and community. The music resonated deeply, and the words spoken by pastor Joey seemed to echo within me, inviting me to pause and reflect on my own spiritual journey. As I stood there, surrounded by Dennis, Roxanne, Carlo, and Aeron, I couldn't help but feel a profound sense of gratitude for the friendships we had built over the years. These were the kind of bonds that could only be formed through shared experiences, trust, and genuine love. At that moment, I found myself reflecting not only on the present but on everything that had led me to this place: my trip to Canada, the deepening of my relationship with Aunt Leony, and the decision to join Roxanne's family at church. I realized that all of these experiences had woven together to create a tapestry of belonging and purpose. It was a powerful reminder that sometimes, the most meaningful connections and experiences arise when we step outside our comfort zones and open ourselves up to new possibilities.

The service came to an end, but the peace and sense of belonging stayed with me long after we left the church. I felt more connected than ever, not only to Roxanne's family but to something greater, something that transcended our daily lives. It was one of those rare moments when you know that you're exactly where you're supposed to be.

Before the end of the service, we participated in a breakout activity where we shared our experiences and reflections based on the questions displayed on the slides. It was a chance for us to dive deeper into our thoughts and connect with others in a more personal way. During the session, we met some amazing people—Joseph, Noel, Jay, and John Carlo, one of the leaders of the discipleship group, who had posted the questions for our discussion. As we shared our thoughts and listened to others, I realized that this moment was about more than just the words we were speaking. It was about the connections we were making, the vulnerability we were showing, and the collective wisdom we were exchanging. The experience felt deeply enriching and reinforced my belief that spiritual and emotional growth often comes from these shared moments of openness. I knew, by the time the activity ended, that this wasn't just a simple act of kindness or a way to pass the time—it was a meaningful step in building stronger bonds with the people we cherish. It was about deepening our connections with others, both spiritually and personally, and creating lasting memories that would stay with us long after the evening had ended.

After the service, JC, one of the discipleship group leaders, invited Dennis and me to join their discipleship group, which was made up of other single men. He also shared his contact information with us and extended a warm invitation to their fellowship night, which they held every Thursday at Wendy's Burger near Emirates Towers Metro Station.

At first, I felt hesitant. Although I wanted to connect with the group, a part of me was afraid. I worried that my disabilities would set me apart, that I might be treated differently or even be discriminated against. I've had my fair share of experiences where I felt like an outsider, and I wasn't sure how I'd be received in this new environment. But JC and the other members of the group completely erased those doubts. When we arrived at the fellowship night, they welcomed us with open arms and genuine smiles. It was a reminder of how important it is to be accepted for who you truly are, and in that moment, all my fears melted away. They treated me with kindness and respect, and I quickly realized that, in this group, there was no room for judgment—only love, support, and a shared desire to grow spiritually. Their acceptance was humbling. It reminded me that the true essence of community isn't about perfection or fitting a certain mold—it's about being real with one another and offering support through life's challenges. I felt encouraged, knowing that I was accepted not despite my disabilities, but as I am, just like everyone else in the group.

As the evening went on, I began to feel more at home. The fellowship was warm, the conversations were inspiring, and the connections I made that night felt genuine. Dennis and I both agreed that this would be a great opportunity to deepen our faith and connect with others who were on a similar spiritual journey. What started as a simple invitation became something far more meaningful. I no longer felt like an outsider—I felt like I was exactly where I was meant to be. As I continued attending the fellowship nights, I had the privilege of meeting some amazing new friends. I met Henry, a newcomer from Dubai who recently got a job at a specialty therapy center for childcare, where he applies his background as a psychology graduate.

I also met Mark Joseph, a 27-year-old IT professional and Henry's best friend since childhood. Mark demonstrated maturity in both his words and actions during our sessions. There was Oliver, an aircraft mechanic working in one of the famous airlines in UAE, who has been in Dubai for two years and possesses a generous spirit. Gideon, an accountant at a private company in Dubai for several months now, also has a passion for guiding followers of Elevate at CCF Dubai. I also met Jandel, who has been in Dubai for quite a while and works as the head of the accounting department in his company. He has been facing personal struggles due to the recent loss of his grandparent. Joseph, whom I met during my first visit to CCF Dubai, has also been in Dubai for a long time. He is a promising businessman who is planning to start his own business here. Then there was Allen, whom I've met only once, but he showed strong camaraderie with the group. Anthony, a tall guy like a basketball player, has been active at CCF for a long time. His brother, who also looks like him, is also involved in the church as one of the leaders. I also met Justin, a friendly guy from Negros island, who works in Supermarket. He often joins fellowship nights, despite his work conflicts. Lastly, there's Andrew, a good friend and brother to me, who shared many stories about his struggles—both with his foster parents and his biological parents. He also spoke about the challenges he faces in Dubai as an independent person.

Every Thursday night became something I looked forward to with excitement and anticipation. It wasn't just about getting together to hang out—it was about diving deeper into our faith, sharing our personal stories, and learning how Jesus was working in each of our lives. The conversations were rich and meaningful, and I was constantly amazed by how each person's journey had shaped their understanding of faith. It was humbling to hear the struggles and victories that each of us had faced, and how Jesus had made a difference in every story.

As the weeks passed, I felt more and more connected to this group of men. What started as casual acquaintances soon blossomed into true friendships. We were all united by a shared purpose: to grow in our relationship with God and support one another in our spiritual journeys. These Thursday nights became a source of joy and spiritual renewal, and each week I left feeling more inspired and encouraged. I could see how, through these simple gatherings, we were becoming more than just a group of friends—we were a community, bound together in faith.

My spiritual journey had been smooth and filled with life, but as with all paths, there came a moment that would truly test my faith. In the middle of August, a serious conflict erupted between Tin, Arlie, and Seraphina. It was a fight born of personal issues, but it was exacerbated by something deeper—money. As I stood witness to their escalating arguments, I found myself caught in the middle, feeling like a bouncing rock tossed from side to side. The more I learned, the more I realized that Seraphina was fabricating stories to drive a wedge between the friendships, and at the heart of it all was money.

One evening, things took a turn for the worse. Kuri and Seraphina came over to our apartment, and before I knew it, they were shouting at each other—voices raised, emotions running high. The boundaries between Dennis, me, and them seemed to vanish in an instant. Seraphina became particularly disrespectful, yelling and accusing Kuri with bitterness. I felt overwhelmed, my body tense and my hands shaking. I could feel the anxiety rising in me, a familiar pressure building up, and I feared I might have an anxiety attack. At that moment, though, something inside me shifted. I heard a quiet whisper in my mind—an urging to pray. It was as though Jesus was calling me to respond with calm, not anger or fear. I closed my eyes for a brief moment, quietly asking for guidance. I prayed silently, asking God for the strength to handle this situation with grace.

As soon as I did, I felt a wave of peace wash over me, and I was able to speak to them with calmness and clarity. I asked them to take a step back and breathe, to respect one another even in the midst of their anger. I thought that night would be the turning point, that the conflict would be resolved, and that we could move forward. But just a few days later, more revelations came to light. Seraphina, it seemed, had been spreading false accusations against Kuri and others in our circle, continuing to stir up tension—all because of money. She had manipulated the situation to cause division, and the impact of her actions was spreading further than I had anticipated. Dennis, too, was dragged into the mess. As our business dealings were involved, it became increasingly difficult for him to collect payments from Seraphina and her family. The financial issues only added to the strain, making everything feel more complicated and painful. It was a challenging time for both of us, as we navigated the tension not only in our friendships but also in our business. The situation felt like a weight pressing down on us, and we were both trying to find the best way forward.

A few weeks later, Dennis decided to visit his main office in San Ramon, California, not only for a business trip but also to take a break from the tension caused by the ongoing conflict with Seraphina. I was invited to join him on this trip, and we also reached out to our best friend, Nerissa, who was working at the University of California Hospital in San Diego. During our conversation, Nerissa kindly offered to help me with something I hadn't considered before—she suggested that I get my eyes checked and try some of the advanced retinal technology available in the United States.

At first, I was hesitant. Doubts crept into my mind—how would I get clearance from my doctor in Dubai, and how could I possibly secure an appointment at UCSD? It seemed like a daunting task, and I wasn't sure how to make it happen. But Nerissa's determination and the continued blessings from God worked in ways I hadn't imagined. With her help and a little miracle along the way, I was able to secure a special booking with one of the top retina surgeons at UCSD. I was overwhelmed by the efforts of Dennis and Nerissa. Their support meant the world to me, and I couldn't wait to share the good news with my mother and our prayer group back in Cebu. I knew that God's hand was at work in this process, and I was grateful for the opportunity to take this step in my journey toward healing.

On September 21st, Dennis and I boarded our flight from Dubai to New York, where we spent a few days before continuing on to California. During our stay in New York City, I had the chance to meet my Aunt Aida, my mother's first cousin, who had lived in the city for decades. We went straight to her apartment from the airport, and when we arrived, we were taken aback by what we found. At 84 years old, Aunt Aida was living alone. Her husband and two children had passed away, and she was now spending her days in a small, modest apartment, waiting for relief goods and free medicines from the government. As we sat down to talk with her, I could feel the deep pain in her heart. She spoke with a sense of anger and sorrow towards God for all the loss she had experienced. I listened carefully, trying to understand her grief, but the words seemed inadequate in the face of her suffering. I didn't know what to say, but I knew one thing for sure—I had to pray for her. I took her hand, and before we left, I gave her a tight hug, whispering that God would never leave her alone.

The moment we stepped out of her apartment, I looked back, and I saw Aunt Aida, tears streaming down her face. It broke my heart to see her in so much pain, but I prayed that my words—though simple—would bring her some comfort. In that moment, I realized the weight of life's challenges. Sometimes, we go through seasons of loss and pain that feel unbearable, but God's presence is always there, even when we can't see it. I prayed for her as we left, trusting that God would continue to watch over her, no matter how difficult the road ahead seemed.

After our brief visit to Aunt Aida's apartment in Staten Island, we headed to Manhattan, where we stayed for three days. It felt surreal to be in such an iconic city, and every moment seemed like a dream come true. During our time in New York, we explored some of the most famous landmarks that I had only ever seen in postcards before—places I never imagined I'd get to visit in person. We walked through the neon lights of Times Square, marveled at the elegance of Madison Avenue, and stood in awe before the majestic Rockefeller Center. We visited Broadway and took in the vibrant energy of the theater district, even if we didn't have time to catch a show. We walked across the Brooklyn Bridge, a symbol of resilience and beauty, and explored Battery Park, where the Statue of Liberty stood tall in the distance—an enduring symbol of freedom and hope. I couldn't help but be amazed at the history and grandeur of these places. What was once just a picture on a postcard was now a reality, and the experience left me speechless.

After our unforgettable time in New York, we flew straight to San Francisco, where we were greeted at the airport by my cousin Liezel and her family. It had been a long time since we last reconnected, and it felt so good to see them again. We headed to one of the Filipino restaurants in the city for lunch, sharing stories and catching up on life. It felt like no time had passed at all, as if we had just seen each other yesterday. After lunch, we took a tour of the city, visiting places like Lombard Street, known for its winding turns, and the bustling Pier 39, where the sea lions rest on the docks. Of course, we couldn't miss the iconic Golden Gate Bridge, which stood proudly against the foggy skyline. I couldn't help but feel a sense of gratitude as I stood there, taking in the beauty of the bridge and the city. It was a reminder of how far I had come, not just physically but in my spiritual journey as well. Every moment of this trip, from the busy streets of New York to the calm beauty of San Francisco, was filled with wonder and new experiences. It was more than just sightseeing; it was a reminder of the blessings in my life, the people I had met, and the opportunities to grow and connect with the world around me.

We stayed in San Francisco for three days, and while we were there, we ran into a scheduling issue with my doctor at UCSD. My appointment was set for 3:00 PM, which conflicted with our original flight time from San Francisco to San Diego. Our flight was supposed to leave at 3:00 PM, but we wouldn't arrive in San Diego until 4:00 PM—well after my scheduled appointment. I was feeling stressed, but I took a moment to pray and surrender the whole situation to God. I trusted that He would make a way, even if it seemed impossible. And just as I had hoped, God worked things out. Dennis was able to change our flight to an earlier time, 11:00 AM, with only a minimal cost. I couldn't believe how smoothly everything worked out. When we told Nerissa about the change, she was so relieved and happy to hear that we would be able to make my appointment on time. While we were in San Francisco, Dennis and I also took the opportunity to visit his head office in San Ramon. During our visit, I had the pleasure of meeting two wonderful women from the company, Maria and Rose, who had both been with the company for decades. Maria and Rose were not only great company but also wine enthusiasts, and they were eager to show us around Napa Valley. Rose drove us to Napa, where we visited several wineries, including the renowned Sterling Vineyards. The experience was nothing short of amazing. The scenic views, the exquisite wines, and the warm hospitality made me feel like a VIP. It was a wonderful, almost surreal experience, and I couldn't help but feel grateful for the opportunity to take in such beauty. Maria and Rose were also kind enough to offer words of encouragement and support for my upcoming eye check-up at UCSD. They even prayed for the success of the appointment, which touched me deeply. Their kindness and positive energy were truly uplifting, and I felt blessed to have crossed paths with them.

Our time in San Francisco, San Ramon, and Napa was brief, but it was packed with unforgettable moments. From the breathtaking scenery of Napa Valley to the genuine kindness of our new friends, the trip was not only a refreshing break but also a reminder of how God works in mysterious and beautiful ways. Even amidst the chaos of scheduling conflicts and travel challenges, I couldn't help but feel an overwhelming sense of peace and gratitude.

On September 26, we finally arrived in San Diego, earlier than expected—before noon. Nerissa was there at the airport to greet us, and she took us to a nearby restaurant in La Jolla for a quick meal before heading to the UCSD Eye Clinic. I was both nervous and hopeful as we made our way to the clinic, knowing that this visit could be a crucial turning point in my journey toward recovery.

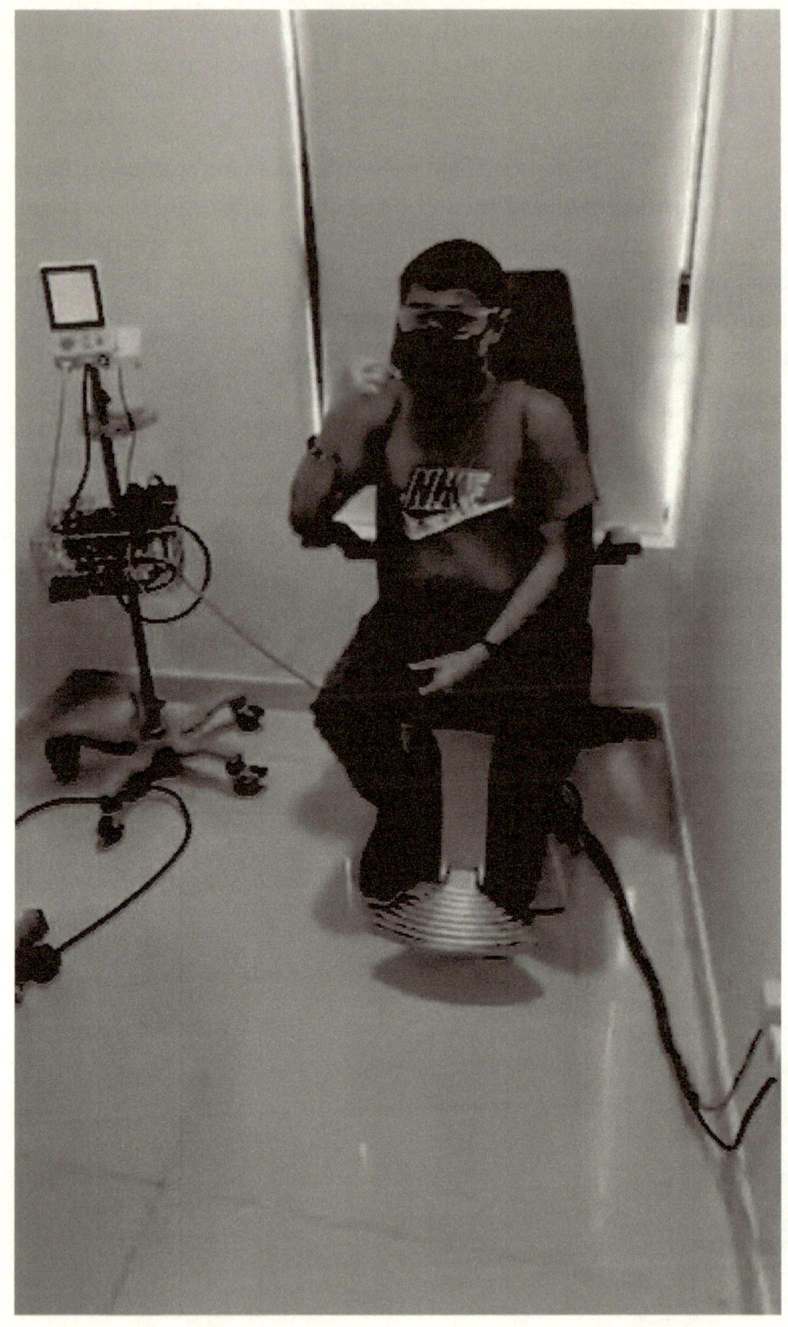

When we arrived at the eye specialty clinic, Nerissa helped us get the initial quotation from the doctor. The estimate for the full tests and check-up came to approximately $3,000, which was a significant amount. I quietly prayed to God, asking for His help with the financial burden, knowing that we couldn't afford that kind of cost. As I sat there waiting for my turn, I tried to stay calm, trusting that God would provide a way. A few minutes later, something incredible happened. One of the clinic staff approached us and informed us that the total cost would only be $1,500—half of the original quotation.

While I felt some relief, I couldn't shake the feeling that God was still working behind the scenes. I prayed once again, asking Jesus Christ for even more of a blessing—knowing that nothing is impossible with Him. Soon after, one of the nurses called me in for laboratory tests, and after the examination, I finally got to meet Dr. Christopher, one of the top retina surgeons at UCSD. I shared my entire medical history with him, including the details from my doctors in the Philippines and Dubai, which he carefully reviewed and added to my medical file. After analyzing my condition, Dr. Christopher gave me the incredible news: there was a chance for me to regain my vision. However, the process would take time—it could take anywhere from six months to a year, as the silicone oil in my eyes would need to be removed, and some blood clots that were causing my blurry vision would have to be addressed. As we continued our conversation, Nerissa asked Dr. Christopher about the overall cost of the operation, including follow-up check-ups and medication. Dr. Christopher was incredibly kind and said that we could request a breakdown of the costs from the clinic staff. But what truly stunned me was when he mentioned that I could apply for financial aid through the University's Charity Institution. I was in disbelief. It was as though God was opening a door I hadn't even considered. Not only did I have a chance at restoring my vision, but there might be a way to make the costs more manageable. The only lingering doubt in my heart was the reality that I would likely need to stay in San Diego for six months to a year for the treatment and follow-ups. It was a significant commitment, and part of me felt overwhelmed by the thought of being away from home for so long. But despite my worries, I could see God's hand at work in every detail, providing a way forward when I had almost lost hope. After the consultation, the clinic staff provided us with the final bill. God's provision was evident once again—when I heard the amount, I could hardly believe it. Instead of the

$1,500 I had anticipated, the total cost came to around $500. I was in awe of God's generosity and timing. It was a reminder that even in moments of uncertainty, God's plan is always greater than our own.

We stayed in San Diego for five more days before heading back to Dubai. Our time in the city was filled with gratitude, as our primary mission—seeing my doctor at UCSD—had been successful, and we were also able to spend quality time with my best friend Nerissa, her husband John, their son JJ, and the rest of their family. It was a blessing to reconnect with them after so long, and we made the most of our time together, sharing stories, laughs, and memories.

During our stay, we also visited some wonderful places in and around San Diego, including a trip to Anaheim. There, we had the chance to meet up with Alona, one of our friends from Dubai, who was now living in California with her mother. It had been a while since we'd seen her, and it was great to catch up. Over a lunch date, Alona shared with us some stories that shed more light on the situation with Seraphina. She validated many of the things we had suspected about Seraphina's behavior, which helped us better understand the dynamics of what had been happening back in Dubai. It was painful to hear, but in a way, it was a relief to finally get clarity.

The whole trip, despite the challenges and emotional moments, was a reminder of how important relationships are. From the blessings of medical care to the comfort of good friends and family, I felt God's presence in every aspect of our journey. It was a time of healing, both physically and emotionally, and a chance to reflect on how far I had come. As we prepared to return to Dubai, I couldn't help but feel a deep sense of peace, knowing that God had been guiding us every step of the way.

A few days after our arrival in Dubai, I had a dream that stayed with me long after I woke up. In the dream, I was sitting on a couch in a house that felt familiar—Aline's place in Marikina. Her mother was sitting next to me, holding my hands, and she said, "You need to talk to Aline." Her words were so clear and direct, and they lingered in my mind long after I awoke. I knew that I had to do something about it, but I wasn't sure what. When I shared the dream with Dennis, he was immediately excited. He suggested that we reach out to Aline right away. But I hesitated. There was still a part of me that was reluctant to call her. My doubts were rooted in the painful words Seraphina had said to me—that Aline didn't want to have anything to do with me, that she was discriminating against my disabilities. Those words had caused a lot of hurt, and they still echoed in my heart, making me unsure whether reaching out was the right thing to do. Days passed, and I struggled with the decision. But during one of our discipleship fellowship nights with JC and the other single men, our discussion centered on the topics of salvation and forgiveness. As we talked about letting go of past pain and the importance of forgiving those who had hurt us, I realized something profound: I needed to let go of the bitterness and anger I had been holding onto—not just towards Aline, but towards everyone who had caused me pain. I understood that forgiveness wasn't just for them—it was for me, too. It was the only way to heal and move forward. The next morning, I decided it was time to act. I asked Dennis to assist me in dialing Aline's number on my phone. My heart was racing, but I knew I had to take this step. When Aline picked up, I took a deep breath and told her, "I saw your mother in my dream. She told me I need to talk to you." It was surprising to hear her voice again, and I could feel the warmth and familiarity in her tone, something I hadn't realized I'd missed. Aline was also surprised by my call, but she was open and kind, and we talked for a while. She mentioned that she would be returning from a trip to Kazakhstan soon, and she wanted to meet up after that. I was filled with a mixture of emotions—relief, joy, and even a little nervousness—but most of all, I felt a sense of peace. The walls that had stood between us seemed to be crumbling, and I knew that God had used that dream to open the door to healing and reconciliation.

A week later, we finally met with Aline, along with Sally, Ruby, Yani, and Dennis. We visited Aline's apartment near Emirates Towers Metro Station, and I felt an immediate sense of sincerity and warmth as we entered her home. That day turned out to be a day of revelation, where not only did I listen to their stories, but I also had the chance to share mine—especially the painful experiences with Seraphina. As we all sat together, the tension that had once been between us began to dissipate. I could see that Aline, Sally, and Ruby, who had all been affected by Seraphina's lies and manipulations, were relieved to finally talk openly about the truth. They shared their own painful encounters with Seraphina, and I found myself nodding along in agreement, realizing just how deeply her fabricated stories had impacted everyone.

After all the revelations from my friends, I came to a painful realization: Seraphina had her own motives for destroying the long-term friendship we had within our circle. The most painful part was realizing that she had been used by others with ill intentions to carry out negative actions against other people, including me. As these realizations unfolded, memories of the past few years flooded my mind, each instance revealing the depth of her betrayal. First, she didn't want me to reconnect with Aline and fill in the gaps in our relationship. Instead, she isolated me, making sure I had no chance to mend the friendship that had been strained. Second, there were numerous occasions when she spoke against me to others, spreading hurtful words and even discriminating against my disabilities. The cruelty of her actions cut deeper than I could have imagined. And the final blow was when she deliberately worked to undermine the trust I had invested in her over the years, betraying the bond we once shared. The weight of these realizations hit me all at once. It was hard to reconcile the person I thought I knew with the one who had caused so much pain. Yet, in the end, I had to acknowledge that sometimes the people we trust the most can be the ones who hurt us the deepest.

Over the years, I've had my fair share of challenges, but one of the most painful experiences has been dealing with Seraphina. I've heard so many things from different people about her actions, things that have truly shaken me and made me question the nature of our relationship. Seraphina has not only made fun of my disabilities in private but has also spread false and hurtful stories about my character and my personal life. It's hard to describe the pain of knowing that someone I once considered a friend and a go-to-sister would speak about me so negatively behind my back. She pretended to be kind and friendly to me, but when I wasn't around, she would say things that were cruel and damaging. I came to realize that Seraphina was actively working to undermine my reputation in the eyes of others. It wasn't just a few offhand comments; she made a deliberate effort to distort the truth and paint me in the worst possible light. What hurt the most was not just what she said, but how she orchestrated situations that would isolate me. Seraphina would manipulate circumstances in a way that made it difficult for others to see who I truly was. I found myself in situations where I was left out, excluded, or misunderstood, simply because of the false image she created. It seemed as though, at every turn, she was pushing me further into a corner where I had no one to turn to, no one who could see beyond the lies.

The worst part is that, when I confronted some of the people who had heard these rumors, they told me that Seraphina had painted me as a person who was difficult to work with, untrustworthy, and even selfish. These false impressions spread like wildfire, and it became increasingly hard to undo the damage. What made it all even more confusing was that Seraphina would act so sweet and caring to my face, making me question whether I was overreacting or imagining things. But as time went on, the truth became clearer. Seraphina's actions weren't just gossip or harmless teasing—they were calculated attempts to destroy my reputation and alienate me from people who might otherwise have been my allies. It was a lonely experience, trying to navigate these complicated relationships while being targeted in such a personal way. I felt as though I was fighting a battle on two fronts: one against the hurtful lies being told about me, and the other against the confusion of wondering who I could really trust. As difficult as this situation has been, it has also taught me a lot about resilience. I've learned to rely more on the people who truly know me and the values I hold dear. In the end, I've come to realize that no matter how hard Seraphina tries to twist the narrative, the truth will always shine through. It's just a matter of time before others see her for what she really is. But even more importantly, I've learned that kindness and honesty are qualities worth holding onto, no matter how much others might try to take them away. And though it hasn't been easy, I continue to move forward, knowing that I have the power to control how I respond to her actions and the kind of person I choose to be.

This kind of struggle is not only a test of friendship and faith, but also a profound challenge in learning to manage my temper. It became a journey of self-discovery, where I was forced to confront emotions I hadn't fully understood before. I was hurt, deeply hurt, by the things that were revealed to me, and especially by how Seraphina, someone I once trusted and considered family, behaved toward us. At first, I was overwhelmed with anger, and my heart was consumed by hatred. How could she treat us this way? I had always treated her as an older sister, a part of the small family I had built around me, someone I thought I could rely on no matter what. But in that moment, I felt betrayed and disillusioned. I didn't expect this from her, not after all we had been through together.

In the midst of this pain, I began to pray for guidance, for peace. I asked God to help me understand why this was happening and to help me find the strength to forgive. Slowly, I began to feel a shift within me. Instead of allowing the anger to consume my thoughts, I felt a sense of clarity wash over me, almost as if God was opening my eyes to something greater. I started to realize that this was not just about what Seraphina had done, but about what I was allowing myself to feel. It was about my own ability to rise above the situation and manage my emotions.

God illuminated the path of self-control, showing me that I didn't have to react impulsively, that I didn't have to give in to my anger and let it guide my actions. I understood that holding on to hatred would only harm me further, and that forgiveness and understanding were far more powerful. Through this process, I learned to pause, to reflect, and to make decisions based on wisdom, not emotion. It was a difficult and painful lesson, but one that I now recognize as a complete transformation of my character. I was no longer the person who acted on impulse or let their emotions control their actions. Instead, I was learning to think deeply about my responses, to consider the consequences, and to choose a path of peace and wisdom.

In those quiet moments of prayer and reflection, I began to see that this struggle wasn't just a test of my relationship with Seraphina, but a test of my own growth as a person. I was learning to be stronger, not by holding on to anger, but by letting go. It was a journey of transformation, one that taught me how to manage my emotions, how to forgive, and how to approach life with a deeper sense of understanding and self-control.

It was clear we all felt the same way about her—her motives were always selfish, and her attempts to destroy people's reputations were rooted in something dark and unreasonable. But as much as we all had reasons to harbor anger and resentment towards Seraphina, that day was also a turning point for us. It was the day of reconciliation. I knew that in order to heal fully, I needed to ask for forgiveness—not just for the pain Seraphina caused, but for the misunderstandings and distance that had built up between me and these wonderful women in front of me. So, I gathered my courage and asked Aline, Sally, and Ruby for their forgiveness for any wrongs I had done, whether intentional or not. What happened next was more than I could have hoped for. Their faces softened, and they embraced me with open hearts. It was a moment of healing, not just for me, but for all of us. That day marked the start of a new beginning—a fresh chapter in our friendship. It was as if the weight of all the past hurt and misunderstandings had been lifted, and we were all free to move forward, stronger and more united than ever.

The struggles I faced during this chapter of my life were deeply rooted in my journey of accepting my disability. I was terrified of being discriminated against, especially by my friends and family, and I was unsure how they would react to my situation. The fear of judgment weighed heavily on me. However, through this challenging period, I learned a powerful lesson: no matter the limitations and imperfections I may have, the most important thing is that I accept myself fully. With God's grace, I came to realize that true acceptance begins with me. It's not about seeking approval from others, but about embracing who I am, imperfections and all, and trusting in God's plan for me. In doing so, I found peace, strength, and a deeper sense of self-worth that no external judgment could ever take away.

In mid-October, Dennis and I received an invitation to attend the *True Life Seminar* at CCF Dubai—a two-day, and a night event designed to deepen our faith and spiritual lives in Jesus. The seminar was held in Al Barsha, and we were both eager to attend, knowing that it would be a transformative experience. Throughout the event, we had the opportunity to meet again our D group friends, including John Carlo, Mark, Andrew, and Oliver. The sessions were incredibly powerful, and I remember how deeply the teachings impacted me. The first topic, about the love of the Father, struck my heart in a way I didn't expect. It reminded me of the love my own father had for me, but more importantly, it deepened my understanding of the unconditional love God has for each of us. This love, so pure and unwavering, became a foundation for everything else we learned during the seminar.

As the seminar progressed, we discussed God's sacrifices, and each topic seemed to speak directly to my heart. I realized how much God had done for me, and how much I still had to learn about His grace and mercy. One of the most significant moments for me was when the topic of baptism was introduced. The idea of publicly declaring my faith and fully committing my life to Jesus became real to me at that moment. We were split into different teams, and I found myself in the Blue Team, *Kamagong*.

The nights were filled with discussions, prayers, and moments of deep reflection. It was a time of joy, but also of profound realization. We shared stories of our struggles and triumphs, and together, we saw the bigger picture of God's purpose in our lives. By the end of our first day, I knew in my heart that I wanted to fully surrender my life to Jesus. I wanted to be baptized and commit to following Him completely. That night, as I stepped into the baptismal waters, I felt an overwhelming sense of peace and grace. As I was submerged, it was as if all my past burdens were washed away. I felt renewed, refreshed—reborn. At that moment, I knew I was not the same person I had been before. I was a new creation, filled with a deep reverence for God and a commitment to live my life in His service. The fear and uncertainty that once held me back were replaced with a firm trust in His guidance.

The next day, we had our final seminar, and the session was led by Jay Ar, a B1G leader who guided us through this unforgettable experience. Just a few minutes later, John Carlo, my discipleship group leader, approached me with a request: "Would you be willing to speak in front of everyone and share your testimony of your experience before and during the *True Life* seminar?" At first, I hesitated. I was afraid—afraid of being judged, of being discriminated against because of my disabilities, and of speaking in front of so many people. But JCwas incredibly supportive. He reassured me that he would be right there with me, standing by my side as I spoke. That gave me some courage, and I agreed to share my story. I was the last person to speak, and as I stood up to take the microphone, I could feel my hands shaking.

At that moment, I turned to God in prayer, silently asking Him for the strength and courage to share my journey. And then, by His grace, I began. The words came out more freely than I expected. I talked about my journey through darkness, how I had faced so many challenges, including my battle with blindness, anxiety, and depression. I shared how, through it all, I had encountered God's grace and love. As I spoke, I noticed that some people in the audience were crying. The emotion in the room was palpable, and before I knew it, I was crying too. It was as though the Holy Spirit was moving in the room, and I could feel His presence surrounding us all. I continued, and it felt like my words were no longer just mine—they were a message from God, reaching the hearts of everyone listening.

By the time I finished, I was filled with peace, and I could sense the inspiration in the room. The tears I saw in others' eyes were a powerful reminder that our stories, no matter how broken they may seem, can touch others and bring hope. As I sat down, I realized that this moment—this testimony—marked a new chapter in my life. It was a moment of complete surrender, a public declaration that Jesus had walked with me through my darkest times and had never left me alone. No matter the trials we face, Jesus is always with us, guiding us through.

After that life-changing event, something shifted inside me. I began to pray for Seraphina and her family, despite everything that had happened between us. The anger and hatred that had once filled my heart were now completely gone. I was astonished at how my heart had softened.

Looking back, I could see that everything had happened for a reason. I had once had a good job, many friends, promising plans for my family, savings, and businesses. But in the blink of an eye, it was all gone.I lost my eyesight, and I had even attempted suicide, consumed by despair. But if I had given up back then, if I had listened to the whispers of darkness and followed the lies of the enemy in my mind, I wouldn't be who I am today. I wouldn't have experienced the love and grace of Jesus, and I wouldn't have discovered the strength and hope that only He can provide. Jesus Christ is our Savior. He is the God of light, the most powerful One. In my darkest moments, when I was surrounded by the storm clouds of despair—like the heavy, looming Nimbus clouds—I couldn't see a way out. But I've learned that behind those dark clouds is the light of God, shining through. And it's that light that gives us hope, reminding us that there is always a greater future ahead, a future that God has already planned for each one of us. If I had allowed the darkness to consume me, I would never have seen that light. But God is faithful. He never left me, and now I know that my story is not just about my struggles, but about the incredible transformation that happens when we place our trust in Him. Through Jesus, there is always hope, even when the world seems dark. **There is always light beyond the dark clouds called Nimbus.**

Thank you so much for taking the time to read my story. May God bless each and every one of you!

Overview

According to World Health Organization

Every year 726 000 people take their own life and there are many more people who make suicide attempts. Every suicide is a tragedy that affects families, communities and entire countries and has long-lasting effects on the people left behind. Suicide occurs throughout the lifespan and was the third leading cause of death among 15–29-year-olds globally in 2021. Suicide does not just occur in high-income countries but is a global phenomenon in all regions of the world. In fact, close to three quarters (73%) of global suicides occurred in low- and middle-income countries in 2021. Suicide is a serious public health problem that requires a public health response. With timely, evidence-based and often low-cost interventions, suicides can be prevented. For national responses to be effective, a comprehensive multisectoral suicide prevention strategy is needed. (source: www.who.int)

As a survivor, I am dedicated to helping people who are facing difficulties in life, especially those who are blind or disabled like myself. I am here to offer support, lend a listening ear, and provide counseling if needed. Please don't hesitate to reach out to me for prayer or guidance. You can contact me via email at wybenn.clark12@gmail.com.

"For God so loved the world, that he gave his only Son, that whoever believes in him should not perish but have eternal life. " John 3:16

www.ingramcontent.com/pod-product-compliance
Lightning Source LLC
LaVergne TN
LVHW091324150826
845673LV00006B/1759